·One Meal·
FOR ALL

·One Meal·
FOR ALL

Gluten Free, Dairy Free, Soy Free,
Intermittent Fasting and Vegan
Love to Cook Book

VIVIENNE PASQUA

gatekeeper press

Columbus, Ohio

One Meal for All: Gluten Free, Dairy Free, Soy Free, Intermittent Fasting and Vegan Love to Cook Book

Published by Gatekeeper Press
2167 Stringtown Rd, Suite 109
Columbus, OH 43123-2989
www.GatekeeperPress.com

ISBN (hardcover): 9781662903380
eISBN: 9781662903397

Library of Congress Control Number: 2020943198

Contents

Introduction

This cookbook is filled with recipes and menu options for cooking, baking and presenting a lovely, easy, fun meal.

Most diet books are exclusive. This *love to cook book* is inclusive. The norm is usually that people with different eating behaviors attempt to eat together and have multiple meals, while trying to satisfy everyone's dietary needs. This is commonplace at meal time in many households. This cookbook is *one meal for all*.

According to *The International Food Information Council Foundation*, a third of Americans are on a diet at any given time. This became aware to me while teaching nutrition at colleges and many years working as a nutrition consultant. Basically everyone I met or worked with was on some kind of eating plan lifestyle or in simpler terms, a diet. The idea to write a cookbook was solidified during the shelter-in-place we experienced during the Covid-19 pandemic of 2020. So, what to make for dinner? Everyone is home and we all want something different. My gluten free, dairy free sister, my vegan niece and my soy-allergy friend. Do you get the picture?

One Meal for All.

We ultimately want food that tastes great! It must be super easy to prepare, while meeting our individual needs. This book addresses the current food trends of 2020; animal rights, personal beliefs, politics, environmental, diets and health concerns, which all determine how we eat and our personal food choices.

Eating and love both start with the mouth. A kiss represents our need to accept love and share love with one another. The fundamental first breath, suckling and nurturing. Food is needed to sustain life and is pleasurable. Feeding others with food is a gesture of love. This *Love to Cook Book*'s purpose is to preserve my loving Italian legacy, where food is love, and the ultimate goal of bringing love into a world where labels and restrictions seem to dominate life. Let us all sit at the table together, letting go of all that separates us as we come together and share One Meal for All.

My term me-gan (a play on vegan) fits perfectly here! It is time we are free to choose our foods, beliefs, and diets. In my university class, you will find me saying, "Don't preach or defend what you eat, it's not about you. Educate and motivate then allow others to choose for themselves." This cookbook was designed to work with the many diets of our time, using cool and fun ingredients and it is simple enough for the new home chef.

Why a cookbook with no pictures? I decided not to include recipe pictures because it dawned on me that most of my favorite cookbooks are the ones without pictures (*The Enchanted Broccoli Forest, Moosewood Cookbook, The Silver Palate, Miami Spice and the Perennial Political Palate*). Those are the cookbooks I want to create from. My cookbooks with photographs, I find myself just wanting to look at them. The pictures-less books leave me with a curiosity to cook. As the picture cookbooks can be intimidating for a perfectionist.

A Literary Hub article said, "Cookbooks are so much more than recipes and photographs." There was also a recent article in the Wall Street Journal, "Dare to Cook Photo Free (And love it so much more)" that also supports the idea of picture-free recipes.

It's kind of similar to comparing a movie to its original book. Isn't the book always better? The imagination usually wins. The home chef should have the power over their product without comparison. When I have cooked or baked using pictures, I always feel disappointed if mine doesn't look exactly like the print. I am challenging you to use these easy skills without visuals. So, go ahead use your imagination and create. I use social media platforms for recipe pictures and I would love to see your creations as well, so please post yours! #onemealforall

ALL PICTURES ARE ON INSTAGRAM and FACEBOOK: One Meal for All.

Dedication

I want to thank my parents, Susan and Valerio Pasqua, for exposing me to wonderful food. We grew up in a modern, American family with roots in Italy and Ragusa, Sicily. I am one of 6 kids, number 5 to be exact. As a large family, we lived in a New York City suburb.

My dad had polio when he was 7 and later became a "Golden era" body builder, then becoming a chiropractor. We grew up on clean eating decades before it became popular. A diet filled with brewer's yeast, smoothies and Vitamin C.

Grandmas Mary and Sadie and great grandma Lucy, had strong food influences in my life. My grandfather, Sarturno was a chef in Manhattan and made delicious meals. When I was in high school, my brother brought live chickens home. I played with them. The next morning, grandpa butchered the chickens, it was a traumatic slaughter scene which led to many years of veganism.

I have three children to thank; James, Tobin and Lydia. Cooking for them was exciting, as it began a lifetime of creativity. The variety of meals needed to feed a family was sometimes a challenge. One liked waffles, one hated waffles but liked pancakes, and the other I'm not even sure, was it crepes?

To my wonderful daughters-in-law, Meagan and Mai, thank you for feeding my sons. Your love of cooking and baking inspires me and has taught me so much. I look forward to your many creations. Then, there's a gratitude and a thank you to my little sweetheart grand baby Mara Jae. I can't wait to teach you and watch you create. It is fun to watch you enjoy grandma's breads with all your funny faces. Our time together is just precious.

A final thanks to Michael, my partner and biggest food fan. I developed every recipe in his beautiful kitchen, from mess to distress to YES!!!

Preface

There has been a battle between food and nutrition over the years. One elevates enjoyment and the other restriction. Specialty diets are not easy to follow. One person generally feels excluded. In this book, my goal is to include those diets and not make people feel they have to be treated differently.

Let us again start this journey with a kiss. Digestion actually starts in the mouth. An enzyme called *amylase* starts breaking down carbohydrates from the food you eat. This combination is called a *bolus* and is what we swallow. Digestion continues in the stomach, turning the lovely bolus into *chyme*. The chyme continues its long journey through the small and large intestines for further digestion, then transportation and finally absorption. Carbohydrates, protein, and fats are absorbed by axillary organs and waste products are excreted. Everything we eat goes on this journey, no matter the diet, the journey is pretty much the same. The body accepts what we eat and manages from there.

In the 90's, I was the town nutritionist. At that time, my cars had custom license plates "NUTRITON" and "UOVER8". One day, at grammar school pickup, I walked past a mom and she said, "It's only a muffin." So, I replied, "I am not the food police." Why do we all have to define or put ourselves in these food boxes? I was guilty of that myself.

This brings me to my university class in Florida. The students there are working towards a degree in alternative medicine and are passionate about health, food and diet. They travel to organic gardens, eat GMO free, buy their meat from ranchers, cook farm to table, and care about the ethical treatment of animals. They share a common thought of better health, a long life and care for planet.

The research shows that specialty diets will be more prevalent in decades to come. So, how are we going to eat together? As a nutritionist, I can't count how many times have I heard this asked.

"I can't eat at a friend's due to my allergy or disease."

"I'm going to a dinner party, what do I do?"

In this age of food availability, let us take dining with friends and family to the next level of entertaining. One Meal for All!

These questions sparked an idea and this book therefore blossomed. How *can* we all eat together? Without defining, defending nor explaining our eating habits. Can't we just all eat the same delicious food? Even if you're not a vegan or eat gluten free, can't we sit and enjoy a delicious meal together? We have enough to divide us, let's not add food and eating to the mix.

Many of chefs will say if you want a great product, you must start with great ingredients. Farm fresh, local, quality, GMO free, organic, buy today cook by tomorrow. Use this rule, whenever possible.

Anyone can make delicious food, but how will you get there? What is your process and time frame? Mood is very important. Whenever I'm not right emotionally or upset, my food will reflect that. Food is love and it shows. I include an equipment section in this book because your tools will help with the process, even though our grandparents and parents made fantastic soups without them. The process time for them took much longer as they had just a knife and a pot. If food is your thing or you want it to be, I suggest investing in the right equipment listed for your long term needs.

As far as nutrition, I decided not to make that my primary focus. However, I won't stray too far away from the science behind nutrition. Let's stick to simple and clean eating, mainly, foods that are cultivated or grown. The primary focus will be on fruits, vegetables and herbs, our main focus *antioxidants.*

How the Book is Laid Out

We will start with an education on antioxidants as these will be seen throughout this book. Antioxidants are our definition of healthy eating and good health.

Next, I'm going to show you which equipment is recommended and then the procedures that help define how to use terms.

There will be a list of substitution ingredients you may want to consider adding or replacing. Read this part carefully, as it will have an important impact on your final creation.

Finally, we will jump into our first recipe starting with brunch and then your main meal which consists of a main dish with a vegetable, salad or soup and ending with desserts.

Super Antioxidants

Antioxidants are compounds that inhibit oxidation. The most common antioxidants are: Anthocyanins, beta-carotene, catechins, copper, crytoxanthins, flavonoids, glutathione, indoles, isoflavonoids, ligans, lutein, lycopene, manganese, polyphenols, selenium, vitamin A, vitamin C, vitamin E and zinc.

In our body, it is the free radicals that do cellular, protein and DNA damage, free radicals are also a part of the natural aging process and are needed to function properly.

Too many free radicals may create irreversible damage and lead to disease. It is the role of the antioxidant to donate an electron to the electron-deficient free-radical, in order to repair the cells and restore health.

Super antioxidants are food items that contain many antioxidants, which are especially important as diets can become very limiting. A super antioxidant is defined by its ORAC level (Oxygen Radical Absorbance Capacity) of the particular food item. The higher the level, the more super the antioxidant's health benefits. Here's a list of items with a high ORAC:

Foods

- Artichokes
- Beans
- Beets
- Blackberries
- Blueberries
- Chai seeds
- Cranberries
- Dark Chocolate
- Elderberries
- Goji Berries
- Kale
- Matcha green tea
- Pecans
- Raspberries
- Spinach
- Strawberries
- Wild blueberries

Herbs and Spices

- Basil
- Chili
- Cardamom
- Cinnamon
- Cilantro
- Garlic
- Ginger
- Mint
- Mustard
- Onion

- Clove
- Dill
- Cocoa
- Coriander
- Cumin
- Curry

- Oregano
- Paprika
- Parsley
- Sage
- Thyme
- Turmeric

Recommended Equipment

Cooking & Baking

- ❑ Baking dish: rectangular
- ❑ Baking/Cookie sheets
- ❑ Bowls metal or glass: small, medium and large
- ❑ Can opener
- ❑ Cutting boards
- ❑ Knives set
- ❑ Mason jars
- ❑ Measuring cups
- ❑ Measuring spoons
- ❑ Pastry brush
- ❑ Peeler
- ❑ Potholders
- ❑ Ramekins
- ❑ Rectangular pan: large
- ❑ Serving Bowls: large and small
- ❑ Serving Plates: large
- ❑ Spatulas: rubber and metal
- ❑ Spoons: large wooden, ladle, slotted and metal
- ❑ Storage containers
- ❑ Strainer
- ❑ Tray: large
- ❑ Tongs
- ❑ Whisk
- ❑ Zester

Baking Only

- ❑ Bread loaf pans
- ❑ Bundt pan
- ❑ Cake pans: 2
- ❑ Cookie sheets: 2
- ❑ Cupcake paper
- ❑ Glass pie plates
- ❑ Parchment paper
- ❑ Rolling Pin
- ❑ Spring form pan: medium
- ❑ Tart pan with removable bottom

Cooking Only

- ❑ Dutch Oven or large pot with cover
- ❑ Griddle: stovetop
- ❑ Grill: outdoor
- ❑ Sauce pan: small, medium and large
- ❑ Sauté pan: small, medium and large
- ❑ Wok: stovetop

Electric

- ❑ Blender, Immersion blender or *Magic Bullet*
- ❑ Food processor: small or large
- ❑ Griddle: electric (optional)
- ❑ Microwave (optional)
- ❑ Mixer, or hand mixer
- ❑ Rice Cooker (optional)
- ❑ Wok: electric (optional)

Procedures

Al Dente
Cook pasta until it is a bit firm in the inside or when bitten into.

Bain Marie
Also called a water bath, consists of any heatproof dish of food that's set directly in a larger, shallow container of boiling, simmering or hot water. Used mostly with chocolate or eggs.

Blend
With a rubber spatula or large spoon mix gently by folding over ingredients, usually just until all is combined.

Fold
A technique used to gently combine light ingredients with heavier ones. Just fold over until blended, avoid over mixing.

Sauté
Move ingredients in oil around quickly with a large spoon or metal spatula. Do not use rubber in hot pots.

Simmer
After a pot of liquid is boiling (many bubbles), reduce heat to a low level (tiny bubbles). Check often.

Mix
Combine or put together to form one substance or mass. In baking, when I use "mix", it's just until the ingredients are blended. Do not over mix!

Toothpick test

Used in baking. When the timer goes off, leave the pan in the oven, open the door, and using potholders, pull out shelf. Stick a toothpick into the center of item. Pull tooth pick out. If there is batter on the toothpick, the item is uncooked inside and needs more baking time. If the toothpick comes out clean, your product is done! *For additional baking time, start with intervals of 2-3 additional minutes and recheck with the toothpick.

Substitution Ingredients

There are scientific reasonings behind why particular ingredients are used in recipes, especially in baking. Liquids substitute for liquids and solids substitute for solids. There is a reason for salt, sugar, eggs etc. So, don't omit these, but use healthy substitutes. An example, in baking would be if you add maple syrup for sugar you may have to reduce the liquid somewhere else because we are looking for similar consistencies to the original batter or product.

In my college days, during an "Experimental Foods" class, we would have five prep stations set up. We would each bake a different version of the same item, such as brownies. One station had the original brownie recipe, the control. The next stations had brownies without salt, brownies without sugar, brownies without eggs and brownies without baking soda, etc. After baking, we had to taste test and record our results. We used a spittoon to spit out the product after we tasted it, as some were just terrible. The results were interesting, and further solidified the importance of accurate ingredient measuring when baking or cooking.

When substituting ingredients, I will rarely give brand names as they and their ingredients change frequently, which could potentially mislead the reader.

Acronyms

GF - Gluten Free
DF/ND - Dairy Free/Non Dairy
EF - Egg Free

GF - Gluten free:
Gluten is the part of wheat it gives it the gluey stickiness. So, when baking gluten free, the stickiness may be reduced. I try not to use any questionable ingredients to artificially replace the gluten. I usually just change the gluten ingredient.

GF Flours for Baking:
Wheat, rye or barley…are gluten containing flours. Almond, coconut, paleo flour, rice or tapioca and a mixture of the above works great. I have removed garbanzo bean flour from this list as the smell with yeast in my Crusty bread, made me gag.

I do not use Xanthan gums, as health wise, I am skeptical. But be sure to take note that many already commercially mixed flours contain xanthan gum. Xanthan gum is added to try and mimic gluten flour properties, so check all labels. *If you prefer not to ingest xanthan gum. I would then suggest a flour mix (1/2 almond flour and 1/2 rice) for better results.

**Note: Be careful of the new commercial, gluten free "all-purpose flours" as many have baking soda in them, which will throw off the baking soda levels in the recipes. If you get a horrible taste, this is why. Too much baking soda. I posted this information to a gluten free social media site. One woman told me her pancakes were awful and she didn't know why. I am hoping down the line, manufactures put a disclaimer on the front of their products, "contains baking soda", but until then, check your labels!

DF - Dairy Free Milks:
My favorite milks for cooking and baking are almond, oat, walnut and hemp. You can make your own milks or buy organic prepackaged. I limit the rice milks as there is just too much rice in gluten free, dairy free products because rice is cheap. Processed rice can easily dominate these diets. You can also use coconut milk (unsweetened). There are also recipes that call for DF yogurts and cheese. For these recipes, I use coconut milk yogurts and tapioca cheeses.

EF - Egg Free:
Eggs have an important role in recipes, they have many functions in recipes; nutrition, structure, leaving and moisture. Use the alternative that best suits your substitution and preferences. There are also egg-processed substitutes available, however I prefer not to use these. I rather lean towards using whole ingredients. The choice comes down to individual preferences.

EF Substitutions:
General rule of thumb
1 egg = 4 Tbs EF substitute (solid measurement)
1 egg = 1/4 C EF substitute (volume measurement)

Chia seeds: Mostly for sweet dishes, though can be used in savory dishes. (Similar to flax seeds). Mix 1-2 Tbs chia seeds with 1 Tbs hot water, let sit a bit.

Fruits and Vegetables: ¼ C for each egg listed in the recipe: Avocado, applesauce, banana, prunes, mashed sweet potatoes.

Flegg: Made from flax meal & water. Mix 1 Tbsp flax meal +3 Tbs hot water. Add to a small food processor. Let sit 30 minutes, until gelatinous. Great in cookies. Yields 1 EF substitute.

Vegenaise: Mostly for savory dishes, though can be used in sweet dishes. Vegenaise (store bought): *3 Tbs Vegenaise & 1/4 tsp baking soda = 1 egg. Use a mild flavored vegenaise. If the flavor is too strong it will affect the final product and you will taste vegenaise in your baked item.

Vegenaise recipe
3 Tbs Aquafaba (the water from canned chickpeas)
1 Tbs Fresh Lemon Juice
1 tsp Apple Cider Vinegar
1 tsp Maple Syrup
1/2 - 3/4 tsp Salt
1/4 Mustard Powder
1 C (more or less) Grapeseed Oil

*In a blender, add the first 6 ingredients, mix.
*Slowly stream in oil until its thick.
*Refrigerate for up-to 2 weeks.
*Use in recipes 3 Tbs & 1/4 tsp baking soda = 1 Egg.

Soy Free

I do not use soy products or tofu, as many people are allergic or sensitive to it. Back in the 70's and 80's, it was thought that protein was difficult to consume for the vegan, so soy was everywhere. we now know a complete protein are a combination of beans, rice, vegetables and nuts which are easily consumed, so soy and the GMO's that accompany them are eliminated from this book.

Intermittent Fasting 16/8

The meal format in this book is similar to the European model. Many cultures in history served the main meal mid-day. This style of eating is great for digestion and for those following an intermittent fasting program. For these reasons, we start with brunch, not the traditional breakfast.

Intermittent fasting is easy! Most people follow a 16/8 schedule: Sixteen hours of fasting (no food, only black tea and coffee) and eight hours of eating. This is usually done between the hours of noon and 8pm. Any window of eating for eight hours and fasting for sixteen works fine. Remember to be done before the eighth hour is up.

Example:
Wake-up - Black coffee or tea
12:00 Noon - Brunch
7:00 pm - Main Dish with soup, side or salad and dessert

Vegan

The definition for a vegan is best stated by the vegan society, "Vegan is a way of living which seeks to exclude, as far as is possible and practicable, all forms of exploitation of, and cruelty to, animals for food, clothing or any other purpose."

There are many ways to embrace vegan living. Yet one thing all vegans have in common is avoiding all animal products such as, meat (including fish, shellfish and insects), dairy, eggs and honey, as well as avoiding animal-derived materials such as leathers and animal fur clothing, as well as products tested on animals and places that use animals for entertainment.

Please note

*HONEY: Vegans do not eat honey. Honey is produced from the labor of bees and in some large scale beekeeping operations removing the honey, can harm or kill bees. Therefore, honey is not used in this book.

**EGGS: Many Vegans eat eggs they are referred to as, ovo-vegetarians or veggans. Although from an animal, egg-laying is a natural process that does not harm the hen. Therefore, I have included eggs in the baking recipes. I suggest using organic, cage free, local eggs. Although, if you are serving a vegan, please use an egg free alternative. (Please see EF).

Recommended Common Ingredients

Please read this section carefully as these common ingredients will affect the health, preparation, and taste of your final product. We will discuss filtered vs faucet water, oils for cooking, baking and finishing, salts and of course, sugar!

Water:
I must talk about water. It's important if you can't or won't drink faucet water, then you shouldn't use it for cooking, especially in soups, or any item that will hold or absorb its water, such as rice. If the water contains heavy metals these may be detected in the taste. So, a good rule of thumb: Filtered water for drinking or cooking and faucet water for cleaning or washing food.

Oils:
All oils should be stored in small, dark bottles out of direct sunlight to keep them from becoming rancid from exposure to light or air. You should not, however, keep them in the fridge as most oils contain monosaturated fats that will get thick and cloudy if chilled.

Cooking with Oils

Avocado oil:
High in monounsaturated fat (typically touted as a "good" fat), avocado oil has a smoke point of about 520 degrees,

great for high heat stove and oven cooking, sautéing, baking and roasting.

Coconut Oil:

Has a specific smell, though it makes a great high heat cooking oil. Since it is solid at room temperature, it is better for cooking than baking or finishing. Smoking point of 350 degrees, so delicate baking is acceptable.

Grape-seed Oil:

Low in saturated fat and has a high smoke point, which makes it a healthy choice for all kinds of cooking and grilling. Its nutty but mild flavor also works well in salad dressings or drizzled over roasted veggies. These Oils can withstand high heats without the toxic result.

Algae Oil:

Also a high heat oil, appearing in stores as of recent. Rich in omega-3 fatty acids.

Sesame Oil:

A high smoking point at around 410 degrees. I mostly use it for Asian cooking as it adds a nutty flavor and marries those flavors perfectly.

Baking with Oils or Butter

Almond Oil:

Because almond oil is the lightest of all the nut oils, you can actually use less of it in baking. It has a light nutty flavor. Food-grade almond oil (yes food-grade as almond oil is also great on skin) can be a bit pricey, though for baking, a bottle of this great nut oil is usually worth the money. The health advantages of using almond oil include the antioxidant Vitamin E and monounsaturated fatty acids (MUFAs).

*Please note, those with nut allergies need also avoid nut oils.

Coconut Oil:
Solid at room temperature, great for baking, especially cookies and crusts. An MCT oil (medium chain triglycerides).

Vegan Butter:
In some recipes, I will use vegan butter (soy-free varities) in cookies or crusts since the consistency is thicker and creamier then traditional oils. These butters are readily available.

Finishing Oil

Olive Oil:
The old school of thought was to use olive oil for everything. But that is not the case anymore. Olive oil has a low smoking point, and if heated too high, the oil begins to break down and starts to smoke, so it's not good for high heat cooking or baking. Our grandparents had that can of lard under the sink that they used for high heat and also often reused it. This is also not suggested. All used oil should be discarded. We know better to use olive oils as a finishing oil, which means we finish the dish by sprinkling some on pasta before you serve it for some extra nutrition, or used in a salad dressing where there is no cooking.

First cold press, extra virgin olive oil is what you should look for. Choose oils with flavor! An easy way to tell if your Extra virgin olive oil is quality is the cough test: The more you cough and feel the tickle behind your throat the better the quality. Currently, the best olive oils on the market are from New Zealand/Australia or California (the United States has their own packaging laws). Other countries don't necessarily follow our exporting laws and may mix their oils with low quality oils. When visiting Greece, Spain, or Italy, bring back or send your favorite oils directly home to avoid exporting laws.

*Note:** I do not recommend fats such as corn, canola, sunflower, safflower, peanut, margarine or soy oils. Though some may sound healthy, high quantities are not as they contain GMO and chemical oils (trans fats) and are not recommended in this book.

Vegan Butter:
A very popular product as its very similar to margarine, without trans fats. It is a great finishing product, as it is very similar to butter.

Salts

Cooking
The flat flakes in Kosher salts help the salt stick to food. Pink Himalayan Salt is similar to table salt at 98% sodium chloride, 2% trace minerals, such as potassium, magnesium, and calcium.

Baking
I recommend using finer salt. I don't use the iodized salt for baking as I sense a metallic taste. Don't eliminate salt in baking as it has important functions, one of which is bringing out other ingredient flavors.

Finishing salts
Serving salts, are added at the end of cooking, just before serving. I especially love the truffle salt, as it's not over-whelming yet so flavorful.

Sugar

Sugar is sugar is sugar! Unless it's in its natural form such as fruits, the sugar you use in a recipe is pretty much digested and metabolized the same. It will ultimately depend on your preference. Very few sugars are more beneficial than others, with molasses and maple syrup being a slight exception as they contain some nutrients.

My go-to baking sugar is beet sugar, as it's not super sweet. Although processed, beet sugar is made using a process that involves thinly slicing sugar beets to extract the natural sugar juice. The juice is then purified and heated to create a concentrated syrup, which crystallizes to form granulated sugar.

I do not use cane sugar although it is produced similarly to beet sugar. Producers of cane sugar sometimes use animal bone char, a bleaching agent, to make sugar white. The final sugar doesn't contain any bones, though this should be pointed out for vegetarians and vegans.

Other sugars may be substituted for beet sugar, such as coconut sugar, date sugar, molasses or maple syrup.

If using liquid sugars, such as maple syrup, it is important to reduce the liquid in the recipe. For example, for every cup of maple syrup used, reduce the liquid in the recipe by 3 tablespoons. If the recipe contains no added liquid, increase the flour by 3 tablespoons.

I do not use highly processed sugars or artificial sugars as their sweetness varies and I do not like the associated health hazards. Stay away! In small amounts, sugar is ok. Keeping your portions small is the key.

Brunch

Avocado Yummy Toast
Caribbean Bread
Crusty Round Artisan Bread
Dark Chocolate Smoothie
French Bread Pudding
Green Super Smoothie
Key Lime and Maple Bread
Lemon Poppy Bread
Maple with a Kick
Maple and Chocolate with a Kick
Oatmeal Chocolate Smoothie
Orange Chocolate Chip Bread
Pancake Clouds
Pear and Ginger Bread
Raw Berry Sorbet Smoothie
Spice and Pumpkin Bread

Avocado Yummy Toast

1 Sandwich

This is my Italian version of this popular toast. The tomatoes & garlic can be made days ahead of time and stored in the fridge.

*Note that when garlic is roasted whole it's flavor and texture are very mild and the consistency resembles butter. This is also true for the Pasta with Slow Roasted Tomato and Garlic recipe.

Tomatoes & Garlic

3 lbs fresh plum tomatoes, trim stem, slice thick
2 garlic bulbs (not cloves)
2 tsp thyme or oregano
2 Tbs olive oil
2 tsp kosher salt
1/4 tsp pepper
1 Avocado, sliced
2 pieces crusty bread

- Preheat oven to 250 degrees. Line a baking sheet with parchment paper.

- On a cutting board, turn garlic on its side and cut off stem exposing garlic cloves inside.

- Place on baking sheet garlic cloves up.

- Add tomatoes next to garlic, sprinkle each slice with all-seasoning.

- Drizzle all with oil and roast for 4-5 hours, until dry.

Arrangement Steps

Toast bread
Spread with mashed garlic
Layer with Avocado
Arrange tomato
Add top piece of bread and enjoy.

Caribbean Bread

2 Loaves

This has been a family favorite for years. I had so much fun baking this for my granddaughter Mara Jae. I love you! This antioxidant rich version is great to eat during pregnancy as it's so rich in folate. Extra bananas? Remove skins and add to a freezer container for later use.

Please note: If you are not baking for vegans, you can use organic eggs.

6-7 bananas, ripe or frozen, thawed & drain liquid.
1 C thawed and drained frozen mango (optional)
3/4 C almond oil
1+ 3/4 C beet sugar
4 EF eggs
1 tsp vanilla
6 Tbs almond milk
4 C GF flour
2 tsp baking soda
3/4 tsp salt
2 pints blueberries

- Preheat oven to 350 degrees, oil 2 loaf pans.

- In mixer, add first 7 ingredients together.

- Mix, next 4 (dry) ingredients together with a fork and add blueberries, this will help evenly distribute them.

- Add dry ingredients to wet ingredients, slowly (don't over mix).

- Pour into tins.

- Bake 55-60 min (toothpick test).

For muffins, use a muffin tin with cupcake papers, pour batter in each 3/4 way up, Bake 35-45 minutes (Toothpick test).

Crusty Round Artisan Bread

1 Round Loaf

This bread can be described as Italian meets sour dough. Using beer helps the rising process (Ginger ale can be used in place of beer). Other bread variations include: 'Olive bread' 2 tsp fresh rosemary and 2 C olives, diced, add to blender with the wet ingredients).

Please note: If you are not baking for vegans, You can use organic eggs.

3 + 1/4 C GF flour
1/2 C almond meal
1/2 tsp baking soda
2 tsp baking powder
1 tsp sea salt
1 tsp apple cider vinegar
2 Tbs maple syrup
1 C seltzer
1/4 cup light GF beer
1/4 C olive oil
2 EF eggs
2 1/4 tsp rapid rise yeast (1 pk)

- In a large bowl, add first 5, dry ingredients, mix.

- In a mixer, add next 6 ingredients, mix.

- Slowly add dry ingredients to wet, use a bread attachment on the mixer. Add yeast, mix 3 minutes.

- With floured hands, form dough into a ball, be sure to get all dough together into the ball. Transfer to a bowl, place near stove, cover with a towel and let rise for 1 hour.

- Preheat oven 450 degrees. When temperature is reached, place a medium size cast iron Dutch oven with cover, into the oven. Heat the pot for 30 minutes. Carefully (with potholders), take the hot pot from oven, gently place dough into the pot. Sprinkle top of bread with water. Cover pot and return to the oven.

- Bake for 30 minutes. Uncover and bake an additional 15 minutes. Check if done by knocking on top, should sound hollow. Gently shake the loaf onto a rack, cool to warm before cutting into the loaf.

Dark Chocolate Smoothie

1 Large Drink

I developed these smoothies for clients that just won't cook. Can't beat the taste of this amazing drink. Dark chocolate is a powerful antioxidant.

4 oz dark chocolate
2 tbs hemp seeds
1 C almond milk
1 ½ Bananas, frozen
1 tbsp almond butter
½ tsp cinnamon
Pinch of Salt

- In blender jar, add chocolate.
  Melt the chocolate. This can be done by using a pot filled 3/4 way with water and adding the blender jar to boiling water for a few minutes just until chocolate is melted, take the jar carefully out of boiling water with potholders and cool. The can also be done in the microwave in a glass jar, test after 30 seconds, cool.

- In a Magic Bullet or blender, add all ingredients and mix, until well blended.

- Transfer to a glass and enjoy.

French Bread Pudding

6 Servings

Start this the night before. Cover and refrigerate once assembled. The bread will really absorb the liquid. If you are serving a bigger crowd, double the recipe and make in a large rectangular pan. I used to make this every Christmas eve and then serve it to the grandparents the next morning. A complete breakfast made the night before... in the morning, just make the coffee!

Please note: If you are not baking for vegans, you can use 6 organic eggs.

GF bread - any loaf of French or cinnamon raisin bread
4 EF eggs
2 tsp cinnamon
1/2 C raisins (optional)
1 C almond milk
1/4 tsp salt
1/2 C beet sugar
1/2 tsp maple extract
2 Tbs chia seeds
Maple syrup
Vegan butter

- Oil a square baking dish.

- Rip bread into large, bite size pieces, place in dish.

- In a bowl, use a fork to mix the next 8 ingredients.

- Pour over bread and let sit in fridge <u>overnight</u>.

- Preheat oven to 350 degrees, bake until brown 30-35 minutes.

- Cut into squares serve in plates, with maple syrup and vegan butter.

Green Super Smoothie

2 Large Drinks

Good and spicy, this is an amazing start to the day. Celery is an excellent source of Vitamin K and molybdenum. This drink is loaded with folate, potassium, dietary fiber, manganese pantothenic acid, Vitamin B2, copper, Vitamin C, Vitamin B6, calcium, iron, phosphorus, magnesium and Vitamin A (in the form of carotenoids). Cilantro is a good source of dietary fiber, Vitamins A, C, E, K, calcium, iron, potassium, and magnesium. Avocado has over 20 Vitamins and minerals, monosaturated fats and protein. The lime and vegetables are high in antioxidants. Oregano oil is an antiviral antibacterial herb. Drink this if you feel a cold coming on.

1 C very cold filtered water
1 bunch celery
1 avocado
1/2 bunch cilantro
1 lime, peeled and quartered
Splash hot sauce or hot pepper
Splash oregano oil
Splash CBD oil
1 Tbs spirulina
1 capsules, Aswaganda, (open and discard capsule)

- In a Magic Bullet or blender, add all ingredients and mix, until well blended.

- Transfer to a glass and enjoy.

Key Lime and Maple Bread

2 Loaves

In this recipe you have some choices. Use lime or any citrus DF yogurt. Use extracts or super strength extracts, but just take note the super strength is used in candy making and it will be more powerful.

Please note: If you are not baking for vegans, you can use organic eggs.

6 EF eggs
2 C beet sugar
2 C DF citrus yogurt
1 C almond oil
2 Tbs fresh lime zest
2 Tbs lime extract or 1 Dram
(.0125 fl oz super strength)
2 key limes, juice
2 Tbs maple syrup
3 C GF flour
2 3/4 tsp baking powder
3/4 tsp baking soda
1 tsp salt

- Preheat oven 350 degrees, oil and flour 2 loaf pans.

- In mixer, add first 8 ingredients, mix until blended.

- In bowl, add the rest of the dry ingredients.

- Stir with a fork until just combined.

- Slowly add dry ingredients to the wet ingredients, mix until combined.

- Pour batter into pans, smoothing the top.

- Bake 50 to 55 minutes, (toothpick test).

For muffins, use a muffin tin with cupcake papers, pour batter in each 3/4 of the way up, Bake 35-45 minutes (toothpick test).

Lemon Poppy Bread

2 Loaves

Lemon is a power food! This is my favorite bread. It's rich in B-complex Vitamins, iron, calcium, magnesium, potassium, zinc and manganese. Use zest from approximately 2 fresh lemons. For a sweet cake/bread, cool, remove from pans and spread top with lemon curd or jam.

Please note: If you are not baking for vegans, you can use organic eggs.

6 EF eggs
2 C beet sugar
2 C DF yogurt
1 C almond oil
2 Tbs lemon zest
2 Tbs lemon extract
3 C GF flour
4 Tbs poppy
3 tsp baking powder
1 tsp baking soda
1 tsp salt

- Preheat oven 350 degrees, Oil and flour, 2 loaf pans.

- In Mixer, add first 6 ingredients, mix until blended.

- In bowl, add the rest of the dry ingredients.

- Stir with a fork until just combined.

- Slowly add dry ingredients to the wet ingredients in mixer, mix until combined.

- Pour batter into pans, smoothing the top.

- Bake 50 to 55 minutes, (toothpick test).

For muffins, use a muffin tin with cupcake papers, pour batter in each 3/4 way up. Bake 35-45 minutes (toothpick test).

Maple with a Kick

Makes 1 Jar

In the original recipe, this was made with local honey. This vegan version is just as incredible. My go-to antioxidant spread! This is a favorite for breakfast. Use Vermont pure maple syrup, as it has less refinement and more active properties. Using this food as an anti-inflammatory agent should be done regularly to receive routine benefits. Spread on toast, make a tea! Optional sprinkle with nuts. Great as gifts in little mason jars!

8 oz maple syrup
4 oz ginger powder

- In a bowl, add maple syrup.

- With a large spoon, slowly mix in the ginger powder, a little at a time until all combined.

- Transfer to a mason jar with a tight-fitting lid.

- Stored at room temperature covered, it will last a couple of months!

Maple and Chocolate with a Kick

Makes 1 Jar

8 oz maple syrup
4 oz ginger powder
2 oz cocoa powder or melted dark chocolate chips

- In a bowl, add the maple syrup.

- With a large spoon, slowly mix in the ginger powder, a little at a time, until all is combined. Then mix in the cocoa powder or melted chocolate to taste.

- Transfer to a mason jar with a tight-fitting lid.

- Stored at room temperature covered, it will last a couple of months!

Oatmeal Chocolate Smoothie

1 Large Drink

I love this and developed it for my sister Fran. It's full of nutrients! There's no need to cook the oats, as the mixing will break them down. I freeze all my extra bananas. First peel, then wrap in parchment paper, add to Ziplock bag and freeze for up to 6 months. The salt will bring out the flavor of the chocolate.

1/4 C oats, any variety
1 banana — frozen
1/2 C almond or walnut milk
1/4 C melted dark chocolate
1 Tbs creamy peanut or almond butter
1/2 Tbs pure maple syrup
1/2 tsp pure vanilla extract
1/2 tsp ground cinnamon
1/8 tsp salt

- In blender or Magic Bullet, add oats and blend/pulse a few times, until finely ground.

- Add rest of ingredients and mix, until well blended.

- Transfer to a glass and enjoy.

Orange Chocolate Chip Bread

2 Loaves

This is Michael's favorite! The fun part about developing recipes is combining flavors. Oranges and chocolate pair great together. I add the chips to the flour to coat because it keeps them from falling to the bottom and they are better distributed in the batter.

Please note: If you are not baking for vegans, You can use organic eggs.

6 EF eggs
2 C beet sugar
2 C DF citrus yogurt
1 C almond oil
1 large orange zest
2 Tbs orange extract
3 C GF flour
3 tsp baking powder
1 tsp baking soda
1 tsp salt
1 bag dark chocolate chips

- Preheat oven 350 degrees, oil and flour loaf pans.

- In mixer, add first 6 ingredients, mix until blended.

- In bowl, add the rest of the dry ingredients and chips.

- Stir with a fork until just combined.

- Slowly add dry ingredients to wet, mix until combined.

- Pour batter into pans, smoothing the top.

- Bake 50 to 55 minutes, (toothpick test)

For muffins, use a muffin tin with cupcake papers, pour batter in each 3/4 way up. Bake 35-45 minutes (toothpick test).

Pancake Clouds

6 Servings

For pancakes or waffles, use a large bowl and mix by hand as this will help limit over-mixing. The rising element here is seltzer, as it adds some fluff to these light pancakes making them cloud-like (my mom's trick). I also use an electric griddle because it sits on any counter everyone can be involved. This recipe is especially fun when the kids are involved!

Please note: If you are not baking for vegans, you can use organic eggs.

2 cups GF flour
1/4 C beet sugar
2 tsp baking powder
1/4 tsp baking soda
1/2 tsp salt
1 + 1/4 C seltzer
1/2 C almond milk
1/4 C almond oil
2 EF egg
2 tsp vanilla

- In a large mixing bowl, add the flour, sugar, baking powder, baking soda and salt, mix with a whisk.

- In another bowl, mix milk, oil, egg and vanilla.

- Slowly add the wet mixture to the dry.

- Add 1C seltzer, mix until just blended.

- Add the other 1/4 C seltzer if batter is too thick.

- Heat a pan, griddle or waffle maker, spray with oil.

- Pour 1/2 ladle of batter onto the pan, or 1 ladle for waffles.

- When many bubbles appear, flip over with a spatula, cook until golden.

- Repeat!

Pear and Ginger Bread

2 Loaves

This bread is a bit different. I enjoy cooking with pears, as they are firm and hold their shape. Candied ginger can usually be found with the dried fruit in bulk bins.

Please note: If you are not baking for vegans, you can use organic eggs.

6 pears peeled, chopped
1 tbs fresh lemon juice
5 EF eggs
2 + 1/4 C beet sugar
1 + 1/4 C almond oil
1 +1/2 tsp vanilla extract
3/4 C candied ginger, chopped
4 1/2 C GF flour
3 tsp baking powder
1 + 1/2 tsp baking soda
1/2 tsp cinnamon powder
1 tsp powder ginger
1+ 1/2 tsp salt

- Preheat oven to 350 degrees, oil 2 loaf pans.

- In a bowl, combine pears with lemon juice, mix and let sit.

- In mixer, add eggs, sugar, oil, vanilla, and ginger pieces, mix well, until creamy.

- In a second bowl, add flour, baking powder, baking soda, ginger powder, cinnamon and salt.

- Slowly, add to egg mixer. Mix just until blended. Add pears, mix.

- Spoon into loaf pans. Bake for 55-60 minutes (toothpick test).

- Cool on racks.

For muffins, use a muffin tin with cupcake papers, pour batter in each 3/4 way up. Bake 35-45 minutes (toothpick test).

Raw Berry Sorbet Smoothie

2 Large Drinks

This super drink screams summertime! It resembles sorbet. It is nutritious and satisfying. Full of antioxidants. Berries rule! I freeze all my extra bananas. First peel, wrap in parchment paper, add to Ziplock bag, freeze for up to 6 months.

1 C cold filtered water
8 pieces of ice
2 frozen bananas or 2 fresh bananas
1/2 package blueberries
1/2 package raspberries
1/4 package blackberries
Splash of elderberry syrup
1 Tbs Gogi berry powder (optional)

- In a Magic Bullet or Blender, add all ingredients and mix, ununtil well blended.

- Transfer to a glass and enjoy.

Spice and Pumpkin Bread

2 Loaves

Pumpkin is delicious and not used enough in cooking and baking. Pumpkins contain antioxidants such as alpha-carotene, beta-carotene and beta-cryptoxanthin. High in Vitamins A, C and E, folate, iron and fiber.

Please note: If you are not baking for vegans, you can use organic eggs.

3/4 C almond oil
2 + 3/4 C beet sugar
4 EF eggs
2 C canned organic (~1.5 cans) pumpkin purée
1/2 C almond milk
3 + 1/2 C GF flour
1+ 1/2 tsp baking soda
1/4 tsp baking powder
1/2 tsp salt
2 tsp allspice
1 tsp cinnamon

- Preheat oven to 325 degrees, oil 2 loaf pans.

- In mixing bowl, add the first 5 ingredients, mix.

- In large bowl, add the next 5 ingredients, mix. Add dry ingredients into wet, mix slowly.

- Pour batter into pans, sprinkle with cinnamon.

- Bake 55 to 60 minutes (toothpick test)

For muffins, use a muffin tin with cupcake papers, pour batter in each 3/4 way up. Bake 35-45 minutes (toothpick test).

Main Dishes

Black Bean Burgers
Chili Tacos with a Secret
Edible Flower Spring Rolls
Fusilli Pasta with Spinach, Red Onion & Carrots
Herbs, Flowers, Rice and Beans
Not your Shepherd's Pie with Universal Pie Crust
Pasta with Slow Roasted Tomatoes and Garlic
Ragusa Spaghetti with Garlic and Oil
Ramen Noodles Hearty Style
Ramen Noodles and Swiss Chard
Sicilian Risotto with Artichokes, Fennel and Lemon
Spicy Eggplant
Tempura Pancakes with Dipping Sauce
Yeah Mac and Cheese
Yellow Curry with Rice

Black Bean Burgers

6 Patties

Homemade BBQ sauce can be made and stored in fridge for weeks. These can also be made on the grill pan or grill mat for 4-5 minutes a side. Cook rice ahead.

Please note: If you are not cooking for vegans, you can use organic eggs.

1 Tbs avocado oil
1/2 C pecans
1 Tbs chili powder
1 Tbs cumin
1 Tbs paprika
1/3 C GF breadcrumbs
4-6 Tbs BBQ sauce
1/2 white onion, cubed
1 C black beans, can drained
1-3 C brown rice, cooked
1 EF egg
Salt and black pepper
2 avocado sliced
Red onion slices

- In a blender, add, pecans, chili, cumin, paprika, breadcrumbs, blend well. Then add BBQ sauce and white onion, blend quickly, until mixed, transfer to a large bowl.

- Add beans, rice (1 cup at a time for consistency) and EF egg to blender and blend ingredients. Add salt and pepper to taste. Combine all blended ingredients and place in fridge to harden for 30 minutes.

- Grab a handful of mixture, form into balls, then press center to form patties.

- Heat a sauté pan, add oil, when hot add burgers, 4 min a side or ununtil brown. Remove from heat. Serve with avocado, red onion, lettuce or GF bun.

BBQ Sauce

1 C brown sugar
1/2 C hot sauce
1 C apple cider vinegar
1/4 C blackstrap molasses

- In saucepan, combine all ingredients, and bring to a boil.

- Reduce heat and simmer 1 hour, until sauce is thick.

Chili Tacos with a Secret

8 Servings

Easy, nutritious, kids love this! Especially when you tell them the secret ingredient, chocolate and raisins! The chocolate adds another layer to deepen the flavor. This recipe is for either a Dutch oven or in the slow cooker! (cook 7 hours in slow cooker - low setting).

1 bag dried, kidney beans
4 Tbs avocado oil
5 garlic cloves, minced
1 spanish onion, minced
5 celery stalks, chopped
2 red peppers, chopped
1 large can(29oz) crushed tomatoes
¼ C red wine vinegar
Handful fresh parsley, chopped
Handful fresh oregano, chopped
2 tsp cumin
2 Tbs chili powder
2 tsp salt
¼ tsp pepper
1/4 C DF dark chocolate covered raisins
Taco shells

- 12 hours ahead, the night before, in a large bowl, soak beans in water (add more water if absorbed).

- Drain beans, discard water.

- Heat oil in Dutch oven until hot, sauté garlic, onion, celery and pepper, for 4 minutes.

- Add remaining ingredients simmer (low flame) for 2 hours. Stir occasionally!

- Cool a bit and serve in bowls or in taco shells with toppings.

Edible Flower Spring Rolls

6 Rolls

These are the prettiest spring rolls, great for a main meal. The edible flowers can be grown, purchased online or at a specialty store. They are easy to prepare and have a unique presentation. I do not use soy miso, I use a chickpea version, or you can also use adzuki bean miso, or 1 tsp rice vinegar.

2 carrots, shredded
1 C purple cabbage, shredded
1 avocado, sliced
1 C basil leaves
1 C mint leaves
36 edible flowers
6 rice paper wraps

- Fill a large bowl with warm water.

- One at a time, dip each wrap in water, for 10 seconds ununtil softened.

- Put wrap on a plate or board.

- Add 6 flowers, face down on each wrap.

- Add and nicely assemble the veggies, have fun!

- Wrap it up, short side in first, then roll longwise!

- Serve with dip!

Dipping sauce:

3 Tbs water
Juice of 1 lime
1Tbs Miso paste
1 Tbs almond or another nut butter
Chili powder to taste
2 Tbs white sesame seeds.

- Mix with fork, all ingredients until smooth.

Fusilli Pasta with Spinach, Red Onions and Carrots

Makes large bowl

Can be made up to a day ahead and can last 3 days in fridge, a great addition to a BBQ or a visitor's weekend. Can be eaten cold, room temperature or warmed, it's ready to go anytime.

1 box GF bowtie or other fun pasta shape
1 large bunch baby spinach
1 red onion
2 C carrots, shredded
1 frozen box, thawed artichoke hearts cut in long quarters
Salt and pepper

- In a large pot, add 3/4 full water and boil, add 1Tbs salt, pasta shapes, boil as per directions minus 2 minutes. So, if its 10 minutes, boil for 8 minutes. Drain pasta.

- Add vegetables, mix and cover 15 minutes, (vegetables will wilt.)

- Transfer all to a serving bowl.

- Make dressing.

Italian dressing:

1 C good quality olive oil
1/4 C red wine vinegar

1 tsp lemon juice
1 tsp maple syrup
1/2 tsp garlic powder
1/2 tsp onion powder
1/2 tsp celery salt
1 tsp dried oregano
1 tsp dried basil
1 tsp dried parsley
Salt and pepper to taste
Red pepper flakes,
Fresh herbs for garnish

- Mix dressing ingredients together, add to pasta and serve.

Herbs, Flowers, Rice and Beans

4 Servings

This is a beautiful and unusual dish! I use green tea bags. The garlic and turmeric have many anti-inflammatory benefits and green tea is a potent antioxidant. Most of these ingredients are staples so keep them in the pantry for those days you just don't know what to cook.

4 C filtered water
2 C rice
2 herbal tea bags
2 cans red or black beans
2 Tbs tomato paste
1 tsp onion powder
1 tsp celery powder
1 tsp garlic powder
1 tsp cumin powder
1 tsp cilantro leaves
1 tsp oregano leaves
1 tsp turmeric powder
Salt and pepper to taste

Garnishes

Hibiscus flowers & scallions and/or chives chopped, fresh cilantro

- In a medium pot, add water and tea bags (making sure there are no staples, paper, plastic or strings, only tea bags). Boil the water, add rice and cook, as per directions.

- In a small bowl, mix the spices together.
  In a pan, add the beans, slowly add herbs, spices, and cook for 10 minutes.

- Serve in a large bowl, first add the rice then the beans, add guacamole, garnishes and serve.

Guacamole
1 avocado
1 lime
1 Tbs chopped cilantro,

- Mortar them all together, season with salt and serve immediately.

Not your Shepherd's Pie

6-8 Servings

Make two ways, as a stew or a finished pie. This Shepherd's pie is holiday worthy! Red wine makes this very rich! Grape juice may be used as a substitute.

Stew

2 Tbs avocado oil
2 shallots, minced
16 oz mushrooms, sliced
6 carrots, sliced
1/2 tsp rosemary
1/2 tsp thyme
2 Tbs tomato paste
1/2 to 3/4 C red wine
2 C frozen peas
2 Tbs GF flour
1/2 C veggie broth
1 tsp truffle salt to taste

- In a Dutch oven or large pot, heat oil.

- Add shallots, mushrooms, carrots, herbs, sauté.

- Add tomato paste, red wine, peas, and sprinkle with flour, mix and boil 2 minutes. Add broth and salt

- Serve like this as a stew or continue with the pie.

Garlic Mashed Potato Layer

6 white potatoes, peeled and quatered
6 cloves garlic
1/4 C avocado oil
1/4 C hemp milk (DF)
Finishing salt

- In a large pot, add potatoes and enough water to cover the potatoes, add salt and boil for 25 minutes until soft.

- Drain potatoes and mash (using a hand blender or potato masher) add oil and milk, salt to taste.

- Hold at this step and make pie crust.

Universal Pie Crust

1 Crust

This pie crust can be used for both savory and sweet dishes. In a sweet pie, I would use almond GF flour, in a savory dish, use any baking GF flour.

**Please note - if cooking for non-vegans you can use organic eggs.

1 1/2 C of GF flour
1/2 tsp salt
2 Tbs oil
1 EF egg
1/4 C very cold filtered water

- Preheat oven to 350 degrees, oil a pie plate.

- In mixer, add flour, salt and oil.

- In a separate, small bowl, beat EF egg and water.

- Add water mixture to flour and mix.

- Add more flour if it is too sticky and wet.

- Put bowl in fridge and let dough rest for 30 minutes.

- Transfer dough into pie plate, using fingers, start in center of a pie plate and then press dough spreading it into the pie plate until it covers all the plate up to the rim.

Building the Shepherd Pie

- To the pie crust add the stew, fill almost to the top.

- Cover with mashed potatoes. You want the mashed potatoes to come higher than plate.

- Bake for 45-50 minutes, until golden brown.

Pasta with Slow Roasted Tomatoes & Garlic

6-8 Servings

Can be stored, in fridge for 2 weeks. Whole garlic is much milder than chopped. You can also make extra garlic to use as a butter spread. Use olive oil, in the oven due to a low temperature (250 degrees).

Tomatoes & Garlic

12 fresh plum tomatoes, trimmed remove stem, slice thick
3 garlic bulbs, whole garlic
2 tsp oregano
2-4 Tbs olive oil
2 tsp kosher salt
1/4 tsp pepper

- Preheat oven to 250 degrees, place parchment paper on a sheet pan, add half the oil, coat bottom of pan.

- On a cutting board turn garlic on its side and cut off 1/4 inch of the top (witche's hat) exposing garlic cloves inside. Discard top.

- Place on baking sheet garlic cloves up.

- Add tomatoes next to the garlic, drizzle tomato slices with oil and seasonings, roast for 2.5- 3 hours, until dry.

Pasta

1 box GF pasta, spaghetti or linguini
4 Tbs olive oil
1/2 C fresh, parsley, chopped
Crushed red pepper
Handful of fresh basil
Salt and pepper to taste

- In a medium pot, boil water, add salt and pasta, remove when al dente. Usually 2 min prior to the box instructions.

- Pop garlic out of the bulbs, removing all skins and place in a serving bowl with oil, with a fork mix well, add pasta, tomatoes, parsley, basil and seasonings. Toss well and serve.

Ragusa Spaghetti with Garlic and Olive Oil

6-8 Servings

This beautiful pasta dish is the COVER RECIPE. Must be made with the BEST possible olive oil. This is one of those meals that you can make anytime, with simple ingredients. This is a traditional Italian meal, served all over Italy, though mine has family roots in Ragusa, Sicily. It is commonly made, as a late-night meal, after a night at the opera.

1/4 C olive oil
4-6 garlic cloves, sliced thick
1 Lb GF spaghetti
Salt and pepper to taste
Garnish
Crushed red pepper
1 small garden tomato, cut small
Handful fresh parsley, chopped

- In a large saucepan, add olive oil to cover bottom, heat oil over medium heat (not high heat).

- Add garlic and sauté until golden (not brown) remove garlic from pan put in a small bowl, Hold until garnish.

- In a large pot, add water, boil, add spaghetti and salt. Boil the spaghetti for 4 minutes (it will be half cooked).

- Spoon out pasta from the water using a slotted spoon and add it to the pan of oil, mixing after each add. Increase heat under the pasta to high, add a few spoonfuls of the pasta water if it looks too dry.

- Cook for 4 more minutes, mixing until al dente.

- Add garlic, season with salt and pepper, garnish with parsley, tomato and hot pepper flakes, heat another 30 seconds and serve hot.

Ramen Noodles Hearty Style

4 Servings

During my kid's high school spring track days, the 'track moms" would help raise money for the team. Our #1 seller was Cup-A-Soup. We always sold out, especially during those cold wet March track meets in Rye, New York. For the veggie burger, use the frozen beyond burger (plant based) or freeze extra black bean burgers, defrost and use. I do not use soy miso, I use a chickpea or adzuki bean miso or you can just use 1 tsp rice vinegar.

4 tbs sesame oil
4 Tbs green scallions, sliced
2 carrots, sliced
2 Tbs ginger, freshly chopped
2 veggie burgers, broken in pieces
3 Tbs chili garlic paste
3 Tbs miso paste
4 C vegetable broth
1 tsp onion powder
1 tsp garlic powder
1/2 C canned adzuki beans, drained
2 Tbs cilantro
1 Tbs parsley, fresh
Salt and pepper
Sriracha for taste and heat
9 oz of ramen noodles

- In a Dutch oven or pot, add the sesame oil, heat.

- Add scallions, carrots, ginger and veggie burger (broken up) mix for 2 minutes.

- Add the pastes, broth and spices, turn off heat.

- In another medium pot, boil water, add the ramen noodles and cook as per instructions. Drain the noodles.

- In serving bowls, add the noodles, broth mixture and beans.

- Garnish with cilantro, Sriracha, salt and pepper.

Ramen Noodles and Swiss Chard

4 Servings

Nutritious and healthy… spinach can be used in place of the Swiss chard. I do not use soy miso, I use chickpea or adzuki bean miso or you can just use 1 tsp rice vinegar.

4 tbs sesame oil
4 Tbs green scallions, sliced
2 carrots, sliced
1 C shiitake mushrooms
1 bunch swiss chard without stems, cut up
2 Tbs ginger, fresh chopped
3 Tbs chili garlic paste
3 Tbs miso paste
4 C vegetable broth
1 tsp onion powder
1 tsp garlic powder
2 Tbs cilantro
Salt and pepper
Sriracha for taste and heat
9 oz of ramen noodles

- In a Dutch oven or pot, add the sesame oil, heat.

- Add scallions, carrots, mushrooms, swiss chard and ginger, mix for 2 minutes.

- Add the pastes, broth and spices, turn off heat.

- In another pot, boil water and add ramen noodles and cook as per instructions. Drain the noodles.

- In serving bowls, add noodles, add broth mixture.

- Garnish with cilantro, sriracha, salt and pepper.

Sicilian Risotto with Artichokes, Fennel & Lemon

8-10 Servings

On a recent trip to Donnalucata, Sicily, I had a similar pasta dish. Here is my risotto version. Instead of wine, add more broth or ginger ale. I use a truffle finishing salt at the end for great favor.

4 C vegetable broth
2 Tbs olive oil
1 large onion, minced
4 garlic cloves, minced
1 fennel bulb, chopped
1+ 1/4 C arborio rice
Sea salt and pepper
1 C light white wine
2 Cans artichoke quarters, (drained)
1/2 tsp fennel seeds
2 Tbs lemon juice
1 C ND grated mozzarella type shreds
1/4 C fresh parsley
Finishing salt

- In a large pot, add broth and bring to a boil. Reduce heat, simmer and set aside on a back burner.

- In a large saucepan, add oil, onion, garlic and fennel sauté 5 min, add the rice and mix well. season with salt & pepper.

- On medium heat, add wine, mix until it evaporates (usually a few minutes).

- Add hot broth, a cup at a time, mix until absorbed (~ 5 min per addition) repeat 3 more times until all the broth is absorbed, total broth time is 20-25 minutes.

- Add artichokes & fennel seeds, lemon juice and shreds.

- Serve in bowls, add parsley, season with finishing salt.

Spicy Eggplant

4 Servings

Play with the spice for heat. Use the slender Asian eggplants, as they are milder and have less seeds. cornstarch
is used as a thickener, so it must be mixed into water first.

6 Tbs sesame oil
3 eggplants
4 garlic cloves, whole
3 Tbs tamarind pulp
1 + 1/2 C water
4 Tbs beet sugar
1 Tbs fennel
1/2 tsp turmeric
1/2 tsp cumin
1/2 tsp cinnamon
1/2 tsp cloves
Salt & pepper
2 teaspoon red pepper
1 tsp cornstarch + 2 Tbs water
2 Tbs scallions, sliced
4 C rice, cooked

- Cut eggplant long ways, then turn and cut long ways
  again, then slice into triangles.

- In saucepan or wok, heat sesame oil, add eggplant.

- Stir fry until almost soft, add garlic, lower heat.

- In a small bowl, add tamarind to water and mix, add the
  sugar, fennel, turmeric, cumin, cinnamon and cloves.

- Slowly add the spices to the eggplant and mix.

- Season eggplant with red pepper, salt and pepper.

- In another small bowl, add corn starch to 2 tsp water, mix.

- Bring eggplant back up to high heat, slowly add corn-starch mixture, boil for 2 minutes, turn off heat.

- Serve over rice and sprinkle scallions on top.

Tempura Pancakes with Dipping Sauce

Makes 14

Use sweet potatoes, potatoes, asparagus, red pepper or any other vegetable be creative. This is delicious! A great party dish.

Please note: for non-vegans, organic eggs can be used for the pancakes:

1 3/4 C GF rice flour
4 Tbs tapioca flour
1 1/2 tsp baking powder
1 tsp salt
1 Tbs sesame seed
1/2 C scallions
2 Tbs Vegenaise or EF egg
1/2 carrots
1/2 C squash
1 1/2 C bok choy
1/4 C chopped cilantro
1 C water
3/4 C seltzer

- Chop, spiral or mince, all the vegetables.

- In a bowl, mix the first 7 ingredients together, then add vegetables, slowly, add seltzer and let sit.

- In a small bowl, make dipping sauce, hold for serving.

- Turn on griddle add oil to lightly coat bottom, when hot, spoon half ladle of the vegetable pancakes onto the griddle. When they bubble, turn them over with a spatula.

- Remove from heat and serve hot with the dipping sauce.

Dipping sauce:

1/4 C liquid protein
6 Tbs rice vinegar
4 Tbs water
2 tsp sesame oil
1 tsp red pepper flakes
1 tsp grated fresh ginger
2 tsp sugar

- Add all to a bowl or jar, mix.

Yeah Mac and Cheese

1 Rectangular Pan

An easy mac & cheese dish, popular with my family. This version uses processed ND cheese. The pasta is not boiled first, as GF pasta can get mushy.

12 oz GF elbows
2 Tbs avocado oil
2 C hemp milk
1 bag ND cheddar shreds
2 bags ND mozzarella shreds
1 tsp salt
1/4 tsp pepper
Red pepper sprinkle
1/4 to 1/2 C water

- Preheat oven to 350 degrees, oil a rectangular pan.

- In a large bowl, add hot water, add elbows, soak exactly 4 minutes, drain elbows and pour into pan, sprinkle with oil.

- Add shreds and milk, mix. Mix in Salt and pepper (add hot pepper here for heat).

- Cover with parchment paper and bake (middle of oven) for 40 minutes.

- Remove cover, change setting from bake to broil (high), 3-5 minutes, for browning.

- Remove from oven, taste, add finishing salt, pepper and more hot pepper if desired, serve.

Yellow Curry with Rice

4 Servings

This is based on a Thai dish and it looks like the Italian flag. This is delicious!

1 tbsp avocado oil
1/2 onion, diced
3 garlic, minced
1+ 1/2 C broccoli, florets
1 red pepper, chopped
1/2 C fresh corn off cob
2 C chickpeas soaked or 1 can with liquid chick peas
1/2 C almond or coconut milk
1 tsp lime juice
2 tsp curry powder
1 tbsp ginger, minced
1/2 tsp salt
2 Tbs fresh basil or cilantro sliced
4 C cooked rice

- In a large pan, heat oil, sauté the onion, garlic, broccoli, pepper and corn for 3 minutes.

- Add beans and milk.

- Cover and bring to a boil over medium heat, reduce heat.

- Add lime juice, curry powder, ginger, and salt, turn off heat.

- Cook rice as per directions.

- Serve in individual bowls, add rice then curry, garnish with basil or cilantro.

On Your Side, Salads and Vegetables

Acorn Squash Boats with Maple Syrup

Caesar Dressing

Chestnuts Cooked in Wine

Crispy Roasted Okra and Brussel Sprouts

Crunchy Roasted Asparagus

In Fashion, Macaroni Salad

Mushrooms Stuffed with Kale and Quinoa

Pear, Peach and Flower Salad

Sesame Seed Corn Salad

Spinach with Garlic, Honey and Figs

Temaki Hand-roll Party

Wakame Seaweed Salad with Beets and Carrots

Acorn Squash Boats with Maple Syrup

6 servings

A simple nutritious and attractive dish. Loaded with carotenoids, antioxidants Vitamin C, potassium and fiber. I love to make this savory vegetable on the sweet side. I have also filled the centers with corn or GF stuffing. Fill the center of the squash, sprinkle oil on the top and bake. This is a great Thanksgiving side.

3 acorn squash
6 Tbs maple syrup
1 1/2 tsp almond or walnut oil
1 1/2 tsp cinnamon
Nutmeg

- Preheat oven to 350 degrees, oil a sheet pan.

- Wash and cut each squash.

- Carefully, cut squash in half, creating 2 boats. With a large spoon, remove the seeds and tough fibers, leaving you with a totally cleaned center.

- Put a 1/4 tsp of oil into each boat of squash and rub all over squash.

- Add 1 Tbs maple syrup and 1/4 tsp cinnamon to each boat and sprinkle with nutmeg.

- Place each boat on the baking sheet and bake at 350 for 30-40 minutes, until brown. Pierced with a fork, the squash should be soft.

- Remove to a plate and serve.

Caesar Dressing

Makes 1 3/4 Cups

Use this dressing on salads, raw and steamed vegetables. I've made this dressing for many events. Next to the salad, I have a "Caesar Dressing" recipe card, displayed for distribution, since it never fails that someone asks me for the recipe. My kids love this on raw or steamed veggies.

1 C olive oil, best available
1/4 C red wine vinegar, use a good quality.
1/4 C fresh lemon juice
4 Tbs Worcestershire sauce
4 garlic cloves peeled, leave whole
4 tsp Dijon mustard
3-6 drops hot Tabasco sauce

- In a jar with a lid, add all the ingredients, cover tight.

- Shake.

- Dress salad or vegetables.

- Can be refrigerated for a few weeks.

- Makes enough for 2 heads of romaine lettuce.

Chestnuts Cooked in Wine

6-8 Servings

Not a very popular fruit, which is surprising since chestnuts are high in manganese, Vitamin C, Vitamin B6 and copper. Roast chestnuts for snacking. For added crunch in salads, add to cooked or grilled veggie marinates. Use as a GF breadcrumb (blending them in a food processor). Or serve them in-between courses after the salad and before the main meal. Can use grape juice instead of wine. You will need an old towel. My Grandma Mary made these for Thanksgiving. We would snack on them as we were waiting for dessert.

1 lb (20-30) chestnuts, carefully make a large "X" with a sharp knife, on the top, round side of each chestnut
1 + 1/2 C water
1 + 1/2 C Morellino Wine (Chianti,
Brunello or Montepulciano)

- In a Dutch oven or pot, add chestnuts cross side up.

- Add 1 + 1/2 C water, cover and simmer 20 minutes.

- Add 1 C wine, uncover and boil off liquid.

- Remove from heat and wrap chestnuts in a kitchen towel and place in a bowl. Pour 1/2 C wine over the towel.

- Let chestnuts (in towel) sit for 10 minutes or more.

- Unroll towel and place chestnuts in a basket or plate or serve right out of the towel.

- Place bowl in middle of table, everyone peels their own chestnuts.

Crispy Roasted Okra and Brussels Sprouts

8 Servings

Okra is also a good source of potassium and calcium and is high in antioxidants, fiber, and Vitamin C. The oil from okra is high in good fats (unsaturated) such as oleic and linoleic acids. Brussel sprouts are a cruciferous vegetable and contain cancer-fighting glycosylates. I love roasted okra. I first had them in a Moroccan restaurant while living in Stamford, CT. The flavors are great. It's important to keep all the vegetables roughly the same size when roasting. The taste is so good whether you cook the vegetables together or separate.

16 oz fresh brussels sprouts, cut off ends and discard, slice in half (large one cut in quarters)
16 oz fresh okra, cut off end and discard, cut into similar size pieces.
avocado oil
1 tsp fresh thyme
1/2 tsp garlic powder
1/4 tsp old bay spice
1/4 tsp salt
1/4 tsp pepper

- Preheat oven to 500 degrees, oil a cookie sheet.

- Wash and prepare all vegetables, pat until completely dry with a paper towel (include any small pieces that fall off the brussels sprouts).

- Add vegetables to the sheet and sprinkle generously with oil.

- Add seasonings. Roast.

- Shaking sheet or mixing up vegetables gently, every 5 minutes for a total of 15-20 minutes.

- Remove from oven. Serve in a bowl.

Crunchy Roasted Asparagus

3-4 Servings

Asparagus are an excellent source of Vitamin K, folate, copper, selenium, Vitamin B1, Vitamin B2, Vitamin C, Vitamin E, dietary fiber, manganese, phosphorus, Vitamin B3, potassium, choline, Vitamin A, zinc, iron, protein, Vitamin B6, and pantothenic acid, to name a few. If you can find the purple asparagus, they are full of anthocyanin, a powerful antioxidant.

avocado oil
1- 2 bunches asparagus
1/4 C walnuts or almond puree
GF breadcrumbs
1/4 tsp thyme
1/4 tsp garlic powder
Salt and pepper

- Preheat oven to 450 degrees, oil a rectangular pan or a cookie sheet

- Break asparagus (at their natural break line) discard bottom stems.

- Line up asparagus, in the same direction in the pan, sprinkle with oil.

- Sprinkle with nuts and breadcrumbs.

- Season with thyme, garlic powder, salt and pepper.

- Bake 15-20 minutes, depending on size of asparagus (jumbos will require longer time.)

- Remove from oven and arrange on dish to serve.

In Fashion, Macaroni Salad

4-6 Servings

We sometimes need some comfort food. This is a 2020 spin on the 1950's version of macaroni salad drowning in mayo. Great for BBQ and picnics.

16 oz GF elbows pasta
1 C Vegenaise
4 oz coconut milk
1/2 C wine or balsamic vinegar
1 cucumber, diced
3 stalks of celery, diced
2 lg carrots, diced
1 Basket small cherry tomatoes, cut in half.
2/3 C frozen, green peas
1Tbs beet sugar
4 Tbs scallions, slice
1 Tbs fresh basil leaves, sliced
2 Tbs chives, sliced
Salt and pepper to taste

- In a large pot, add water, bring to a boil. Add a pinch of salt and the elbow pasta, boil the pasta 2 minutes less than the box directions, al dente.

- Remove from heat and drain in a strainer. In a decorative bowl, add the elbows and the rest of ingredients, mix all together.

- Refrigerate for a couple hours, mix, taste to season, serve.

Mushrooms Stuffed with Kale and Quinoa

4-6 Servings

I use a food processor with the chop blade in two separate batches. Clean the mushrooms well and dry with a paper towel or brush to remove any dirt. Mushrooms should be dried before they are filled.

2 Tbs avocado oil
1 shallot,
3 cloves garlic,
1 Tbs fresh rosemary
Salt and pepper
2 packages, large mushrooms, cleaned, stems removed
1 C roasted red peppers
1/2 C kale or spinach
1/2 C cooked quinoa or brown rice
1 Tbs balsamic vinegar
GF breadcrumbs

- Preheat oven to 350 degrees, oil a baking sheet.

- Chop by hand or with a food processor, the shallot, garlic, rosemary, add salt & pepper mix.

- In a large sauté pan, over medium heat, heat oil, add chopped ingredients and cook about 3 minutes.

- Chop by hand or with a processor, mushroom stems, peppers and spinach or kale. Add to the pan mixture, sauté, for 2 min.

- Turn off the heat, add quinoa or brown rice and vinegar.

- With a small spoon fill each mushroom cap with the mixture. Sprinkle with breadcrumbs, oil, salt and pepper.

- Arrange on baking sheet and bake for 30 minutes.

- Remove from oven and serve.

Pear, Peach and Flower Salad

1 Large Salad

This is just so pretty. I prefer a mix of fresh and dried fruit. The flowers can be grown or purchased at a specialty store or online. You will totally impress your diners. The flowers add so much. Always cut bite size pieces for salads. This salad is where you want to break out your absolute best olive oil for the dressing. Use a mix of 1-part vinegar to 4-parts oil, 1:4.

Boston lettuce head, wash and dry, separate and ripe leaves
A mix of fresh and dried fruit -
2 peaches and 2 pears, cut in julienne slices
Salt
1/4 lemon
1 Tbs wine vinegar
4 Tbs high quality olive oil
Spring flower blend, edible roses, cornflowers & marigolds
Organic hibiscus flowers, cut & sifted

- In a large bowl, build the salad in layers

- Add lettuce first, then the next ingredient, etc.

- Dress with oil & vinegar just before serving then add the flowers on top.

- Divide into serving bowls.

Sesame Seed Corn Salad

12 Servings

This dish is delicious and so beautiful, it looks like a rainbow. Serve it hot or cold. I bring it to potlucks and BBQ's, as it can stay out of the refrigerator for a day or two. You can always add in some ice cubes to freshen it up. I serve it in a very vibrant orange lasagna size pan.

1/4 C avocado oil.
2 (16 oz bags) frozen corn or
4 C corn kernels, removed from cob
6 garlic cloves, chopped
1.5 C sesame seeds, toasted
2 green peppers, chopped small
2 red pepper, chopped small
2 orange or yellow peppers, chopped small
2 tsp Salt
1/4 tsp Pepper

Dressing:

1 C sesame oil
1 1/2 C rice vinegar
6 Tbs molasses

- Preheat oven to 450 degrees.

- On a cookie sheet, Add avocado oil, corn, sesame seeds and garlic, roast for 20 minutes.

- Mix after 10 minutes to prevent browning/burning. *Remove from oven and cool on counter.

- In large party pan, add ingredients and mix well.

- Add most of the dressing, mix and taste. I save some of the dressing and serve it on the side in a small bowl.

Spinach with Garlic, Honey and Figs

4 Servings

I had something similar to this at a Spanish tapas restaurant. I was so crazy about it, I came home and played with the ingredients. I love the different flavors. You may want to double it as the spinach wilts quite a bit.

3 Tbs avocado oil
12 cloves garlic, sliced
2 lbs spinach, baby or large spinach remove spine and rip into smaller pieces
6 Tbs molasses
12 fresh figs, fresh or dried, cut in small quarters
1/2 tsp salt

- In a large sauté pan, add oil and garlic, sauté a couple minutes, then add spinach, cover for 2 minutes.

- Add remaining ingredients, mix well, and cover 2 minutes.

- Remove from heat.

- Serve in a large bowl.

Temaki Hand-roll Party

4 Servings

Fun party dish! Don't over stuff the hand-rolls and eat fresh right after making them. I make my sushi rice in a rice cooker. You can use the stove top just follow directions on the rice label.

4 C cooked, sushi rice
1 Tbs rice vinegar
16 Nori sheets seaweed square (3-4 per guest)
Wasabi
Basil
Lemon leaf
Cabbage
Cucumbers
Peppers
Avocado
Red Onions
Bean Sprouts
Sesame Seeds

- Cut all vegetables in thin long slices.

- Make sushi rice as per directions, season with rice vinegar to taste, cool the rice to warm.

- Hand a Nori sheet to each person, hold nori flat on your hand (rough side up) add any mix of ingredients, from lower corner to top corner on one side.

- Roll on the diagonal. (Like a flower bouquet in paper)

Dipping Sauce:

3 Tbs rice vinegar
1 Tbs sesame oil
2 tsp molasses

- To make dipping sauce, in a small bowl, add all ingredients together, mix. To serve drizzle over rolls or dip rolls in.

Wakame Seaweed Salad with Beets and Carrots

4-6 Servings

This is a really fun salad! If I have a sushi party, I make a ton of this, along with rice crackers and fresh ginger. Wakame seaweed is an algae with a strong flavor. It has a worm-like look. It is sold in bags as a dried product. Wakame contains antioxidants, Vitamins A, C, E and K, as well as iron, copper and phosphorus, iodine, manganese, folate, magnesium, calcium and some protein and omega-3 fatty acids.

¾ oz dried or 1 bag Wakame seaweed (whole)
4 carrots, shredded
4 cooked beets, sliced and quartered, cooled

Dressing:

3 Tbs rice vinegar
1 Tbs sesame oil
2 tsp molasses
red pepper flakes

- In a large bowl, soak seaweed in enough warm water to cover, for 5 minutes.

- Wakame will absorb water and puff up.

- Drain, rinse and squeeze out any excess water.

- In a large bowl, add the seaweed, carrots, and beets.

- Stir together the dressing in a bowl.

- Pour dressing over salad, tossing to combine. Serve.

Soups

Amazing Vegetable Soup
Amazing Vegetable Soup II
Beet BP Soup
Butternut Squash Soup
Carrot Ginger Soup
Escarole and Veggie Ball Soup
Leek and Potato Soup with Watercress and Apples
Corn and Hemp Chowder
Pasta Fagioli Soup
Red and Yellow Lentil Soup
Shell Pasta, Pea and Mushroom Soup

Amazing Vegetable Soup

10-14 Servings

Back in the 1980s, my Uncle Cono and I developed this soup for his spa, HRH, in Scott's Corners, New York. I was part of his wellness team. We were the trend! We hosted fasting weekends where a group of clients (some celebrities) would arrive on Friday, and fast all weekend, only consuming herbal tea and water, while they loaded up on spa services. On Sunday afternoon, we would break the fast with this amazing vegetable soup. It really is delicious, especially after not eating for 3 days. A very easy, nutrient rich soup. Prep all the vegetables ahead of time, so you can just add the next vegetable when the timer rings. The long cooking vegetables like potatoes go in first, soft vegetables last.

Can be refrigerated for a week or remove potatoes and freeze. Please note, as you add the cold vegetables to the boiling simmering water, the temperature will reduce so after each vegetable application bring the soup back up to a boil, then simmer.

2 tsp of each oregano,
Basil and thyme
3 bay leaves
1 tsp salt
1/2 tsp pepper
1 C string beans
2 Lg carrots, sliced thick
3 Lg celery, sliced thick
2 white & 2 sweet pottoes, peeled, sliced & quartered

3 tomatoes, quartered
1 zucchini, sliced thick.
1 bunch spinach
2 vegetable bouillon cubes

• Bring 1 quart of filtered water to a boil, reduce to a simmer!

• Add, all the herbs, salt and pepper.

• Add the first vegetable (string beans), simmering for 20 minutes.

• When the timer rings add the next vegetable.

• Repeat this process every 20 minutes until all vegetables are added. After the last vegetable is added simmer 20 minutes, turn off heat.

• Cool a bit and serve.

Amazing Vegetable Soup II

This version tastes delicious as is or puréed, using a hand or standing blender. When using a standing blender soup must be cooled and only fill the blender 1/2 way to avoid burns.

2 tsp oregano, basil and thyme
3 bay leaves
1 tsp salt
1/2 tsp pepper
3 Lg leeks, stalks, cut small
1 onion, sliced
4 white potatoes, peeled, sliced & quartered
2 C broccoli, cut small
2 C cauliflower, cut small
1 C savoy cabbage
2 vegetable bouillon cubes

- Bring 1 quart of filtered water to a boil, reduce to a simmer!

- Add, all the herbs, salt and pepper.

- Add the first vegetable (leeks), simmering for 20 minutes.

- When the timer rings add the next vegetable.

- Repeat this process every 20 minutes until all vegetables are added.

- After the last vegetable is added simmer 20 minutes, turn off heat.

- Cool a bit and serve.

Beet BP Soup

6-8 Servings

You guessed right BP is blood pressure friendly. Beets are a great source of nutrients, including fiber, folate and Vitamin C, nitrates and pigments for health. Similar to borsht, the fermentation of vegetables adds to the health benefits in this soup and how pretty it is! My recipe was adapted from a verbal dictation recipe a family member (Mina) gave me.

32 oz filtered water
2 vegetable bouillon cubes
12 beets, peeled and quartered
2 containers, ND yogurt
2 tsp horseradish
2 Tbs white vinegar
4 carrots, chopped
4 scallions, sliced
4 Tbs chives

- In a Dutch oven or large pot, bring water and bouillon to a boil, add beets simmer 40 minutes.

- Cool completely to room temperature.

- With a hand blender or cool first before using a standing blender, puree the beet mixture.

- Add 2 containers yogurt, horseradish and vinegar.

- Serve room temperature or cooled soup in bowls.

- Garnish with a large tablespoon of yogurt, carrots, scallion and chives.

Butternut Squash Soup

6-8 Servings

I serve this soup at Thanksgiving. This soup lasts in the fridge, up to one week.

2-3 Butternut squash
2 Tbs avocado oil
7 C vegetable broth
1/4 C maple syrup
1 tsp ginger, minced
1 Tbs salt
1 tsp fresh ground pepper
1-3 C hemp milk
Nutmeg, whole grated or a pinch of grounded

- Preheat oven to 350 degrees, oil a sheet pan.

- Carefully cut the squash in half longways, scoop out seeds and brush inside with oil, place cut side down on the pan and roasted for 40 minutes. Cool.

- Scoop out all the squash, discard skin.

- Add squash to a large Dutch oven or large pot.

- Add the broth, maple syrup, ginger, salt and pepper to taste.

- Boil and reduce heat to a simmer for 10 minutes, remove from heat.

- Use a hand blender to puree the soup or cool it well and puree in a standing blender.

- Stir in hemp milk, return to stove. Heat until boiling. Reduce heat and simmer 5 minutes.

- Serve in bowls, with more freshly grated nutmeg.

Carrot Ginger Soup

4-6 Servings

Super nutritious and full of antioxidants. This is dedicated to my son Jimmy, his favorite soup. As a child he actually asked me to make it for him. It is light, tasty and beautiful to serve.

1 Tbs avocado oil
1 Lg white onion, chopped
3 C vegetable broth
1 lb carrots, sliced
1 Tbs ginger, fresh, chopped
1/4 C ND yogurt
1 tsp salt
1/4 tsp pepper
2 Tbs chives, chopped
2 Tbs micro greens

- In a Dutch oven or large pot, heat, add oil.

- Add onions and sauté for 5 min.

- Add the broth, carrots and ginger and bring to a boil, then simmer for 30 min.

- Cool until warm and add 1/4 C yogurt, using a hand blender, or cool first and use a standing blender, blend until smooth.

- Adjust salt and pepper to taste.

- To serve, plate in bowls and garnish with chives and greens.

Escarole and Veggie Ball Soup

6-8 Servings

This actually was Grandma Sadie's recipe that my mom revamped, and then I created this version. I have made this soup countless times, with incredible memories. It was the last meal I had while pregnant with Jimmy. I recently gave the original recipe to my daughter-in-law Meagan to make for her family. So, this recipe has moved into legacy mode!

2 Tbs Avocado oil
3 Cloves garlic, chopped
1 Bunch escarole, washed and ripped by hand in 3rds
2 vegetable bouillon cubes
Filtered water
2 C brown rice, precooked
Vegan meatballs (recipe)
2 tsp salt
1/4 tsp pepper
Red pepper

- In a Dutch oven or large pot, add olive oil.

- Add garlic and escarole, sauté on medium heat for 3-5 minutes.

- Add bouillon and enough filtered water to half the pot or to cover the vegetables completely.

- Season with salt and pepper.

- Add meatballs to soup, turn heat to high and boil, reduce heat to a low simmer, for 30 min.

- Add, precooked brown rice.

- Serve in bowls with crushed red pepper for a kick.

Veggie Balls

Makes ~ 24 Balls

Make a few hours ahead for chill time. Great in tomato sauce.

2 Tbs olive oil
1/2 C onions, chopped
2 cloves garlic, minced
1/2 lb portobello (2 large) mushrooms, finely chopped
3/4 tsp salt
3/4 C vegetable broth
1C GF breadcrumbs
1/4 C parsley, chopped
1/4 tsp black pepper
1 pinch dried oregano
1 EF eggs (Vegenaise)
1/4 C nutritional yeast
1/8 tsp baking powder
1/4 C GF flour

- In a large pan, add olive oil, bring to medium heat.

- Add onion and garlic, sauté for 2 minutes.

- Add mushrooms and salt, cook, stirring until liquid from mushrooms has evaporated, 5 minutes.

- Transfer to a large bowl, add the broth, breadcrumbs, parsley, black pepper and oregano.

- Add EF egg and cheese, mix with a fork, until combined.

- Refrigerate until chilled throughout, 1 hour or overnight.

- Remove from fridge, drain any accumulated liquid from mushroom mixture, can use paper towels to pat dry.
  In a small bowl, mix flour and baking powder, mix into mushroom mixture.

- Shape balls into small round balls 1.5".

- Place on a greased cookie sheet.

- Broil, for 3-5 minutes until brown, use in soup or sauce.

Leek and Potato Soup with Watercress and Apples

6-8 Servings

My daughter Lydia loves this soup. It's her ultimate comfort soup! In fact, it was the first recipe she ever asked me for. As a garnish, the sprouts add a nutty and lemony taste with another layer of complexity. You can serve this hot or cold.

2 Tbs avocado oil
2 onions, sliced
2 leeks, washed and sliced
2 ribs celery, thinly sliced
2 potatoes, peeled and cut in quarters
6 C vegetable broth
2 apples, peeled and chopped
2 C hemp or DF milk
1-2 C watercress
Salt and pepper

- In a Dutch oven or large pot, add oil, heat to high, add onions, leeks and celery, sauté for 3 minutes.

- Add potatoes and broth bring to a boil, reduce to a simmer, cover for 15 minutes.

- Add apples, cook 5 more minutes, potatoes should be fork tender.

- Remove from heat and cool (for blending).

- Puree mixture with a hand blender or carefully in a standing blender (in batches, only filling halfway).

- With a large spoon, mix in milk and season with salt and pepper to taste.

- Serve in bowls, hot or cold, garnish each plate with sprout leaves.

Corn and Hemp Chowder

6-8 Servings

This soup was given to me by a Mexican friend. Her husband owns a restaurant in Connecticut, and this is his recipe. With his blessing, here's my vegan version. So colorful!

2 Tbs avocado oil
5 ears of corn, husk removed, cut corn off core.
1 large Vidalia onion, sliced very thin.
2 vegetable bouillon, cubes
Salt and pepper
1 quart hemp milk
1 container ND yogurt
1/4 C GF flour
Paprika
Chili powder

- In a Dutch oven or large pot, add oil and heat to high, add corn and onion, sauté until tender, 3 minutes. With the back of a spoon crush some of the corn, to release its flavors.

- Add bouillon, salt and pepper to taste.

- Turn off stove, cool a bit, then add hemp milk (or other unsweetened DF milk), add yogurt and mix in flour to thicken, boil 1 minute.

- Serve warm in bowls, garnished with paprika (orange) and chili powder (red).

Pasta Fagioli Soup

8-10 Servings

This is my Sicilian Grandma Sadie's recipe. Hands down, my favorite soup, as it tastes like love. She used to make this for me when I would visit her during my college days in the Bronx. The only difference here is the GF pasta. You can always use canned beans, but I prefer the overnight bean soaking method. This turns out great in a slow or pressure cooker.

2 Tbs avocado oil
1 clove garlic
3 leeks, white only, washed and sliced
2 yellow onions
3 stalks celery, cut small
3/4 - 1 bag dried small cannellini beans
1 large can Italian plum tomatoes, crushed
2 vegetable bouillon
4 C filtered water
Bunch baby spinach
Oregano
Salt and pepper
1 lb GF pasta tubes

- In a strainer, rinse beans, removing any dirty ones, transfer to a large bowl add enough water to cover, let sit overnight or for 8 hours.

- In a Dutch oven or large pot, add oil, heat to high, add garlic, leeks, onions and celery, sauté for 3 min.

- Drain the beans, discard water, add beans to the soup. Add the tomatoes, bouillon and filtered water, boil and reduce heat to a simmer, Cover for 2 hours.

- Add spinach and cook 10 more minutes, turn off heat and add the oregano, salt and pepper.

- In another pot, add water, boil, salt and add pasta cook 8 minutes, drain and hold.

- Serve in bowls, first a scoop of pasta, then a ladle of the soup.

Red and Yellow Lentil Soup

8-10 Servings

This is a recipe given to me by my brother-in-law Kevin. The tarragon is the perfect herb for this soup. You can use, brown, red, yellow or orange lentils in this dish. I enjoy the taste and color of the orange and yellow lentils as they add vibrant color. There is no need to soak the lentils, as they cook fast.

2 Tbs sesame oil
2 onions, chopped
2 leek, white only, washed and chopped
2 carrots, sliced
2 celery stalks, sliced no leaves
1 C orange Lentils, dry
1 C yellow Lentils, dry.
Filtered water
1 vegetable bouillon.
Lemon slices
Fresh tarragon.
Fresh oregano

- In a Dutch oven or large pot, heat pot, add oil, onions, leek, carrots and celery, sauté 5-10 minutes until vegetables are wilted.

- Add the rest of the ingredients

- Add enough filtered water to cover vegetables + 2 Inches, boil, reduce to a simmer, for 30 minutes.

- Serve in bowls topped with a lemon slice, fresh tarragon and fresh oregano.

Shell Pasta, Pea and Mushroom Soup

8-10 Servings

This soup is really something special. A great company or holiday dish. Hearty!

2 Tbs Avocado oil
2 onions, chopped
4 garlic cloves, chopped
3/4 lb Shiitake mushrooms, sliced
3 C frozen tiny peas
2-3 qt vegetable broth
4 tsp basil, julienned
2 pinches saffron
1 C Sun-dried tomatoes, in oil, sliced
1 C GF shell pasta
1 C fresh parsley
Salt and pepper

- In a Dutch oven or large pot, heat to high, add oil, onions and garlic, cook on high, mixing for 5 minutes

- Add mushrooms, mixing for 5 minutes.

- Add peas and broth and bring to a boil, reduce to a simmer.

- Add basil, saffron and sun-dried tomatoes, mix, turn off heat and season with salt and pepper.

- In another pot, add water, boil, add salt and pasta cook ~8 minutes, drain.

- Serve in bowls, add pasta first and then soup, garnish with parsley.

Dessert

1-2-3 Shortbread Cookies

Alligator Chocolate Brownies

Back-in-the-Day Coffee Cake

Carrot and Applesauce Cake

Chocolate Fudge Cake

Fruits and Vegetables Bathed in Chocolate

Gogi Ambrosia with Nilla Pudding

Key Lime Frozen Pie

Lemon and Mint Tea Cake

Molasses Ginger Cookies

Peanut Butter and Chocolate Balls

Pear and Almond Tart

Wild Blueberry Pie

1-2-3 Shortbread Cookies

24 Cookies

Very easy cookies! I remember making these with my kids for a colonial show-and-tell at school. Great to bake with children. Make sure hands are very clean before pressing dough.

Please note: If you are not baking for vegans, you can use organic eggs.

1 EF egg
2 C beet sugar
3 C almond flour
3/4 C vegan butter, softened
2 tsp vanilla

- Preheat oven to 350 degrees, oil a cookie pan.

- In a mixer, mix all ingredients together, in order.

- Place the dough onto the pan.

- Press the dough all around until the bottom is covered with dough, try to get it an even thickness, its ok if it's bumpy, or uneven. Prick the top with fork sprinkle with sugar.

- Bake 20 minutes or until light brown.

- Cool and cut with a knife, in squares and remove with a spatula.

- You can also divide batter, press, and prick into 2 oiled cake pans, bake and cool cut in cake like triangles.

Alligator Chocolate Brownies

16 Servings

Alligator pear is another name for the bumpy skin avocado. This is a great recipe to make with kids as it's loaded with nutrition. When taste-testing I had to tell my people what was in it, in case of allergies, and they were shocked! The avocados give the brownies a creamy fudge texture. For the egg, I use half flegg and half applesauce for the EF eggs.

Please note: If you are not baking for vegans, you can use organic eggs.

1 1/2 avocados, ripe, mashed
1/2 C + 2 Tbs almond oil
1 1/4 C beet sugar
1 C brown sugar
3 EF eggs or 4 eggs
1 Tbs vanilla
3/4 tsp salt
1 C unsweetened DF cocoa powder
1 C GF flour
8 oz DF chocolate chips

- Preheat Oven 350 degrees, oil a square baking pan.

- In a mixer, add first 6 ingredients. Mix well.

- In a bowl, add the rest of ingredients, coating chocolate chips with flour (this will keep them dispersed in batter).

- In a mixer, slowly add dry ingredients to wet, mixing only until blended.

- Bake 25-30 minutes (toothpick test).

- Cool and refrigerate to set, cut into squares.

Back-in-the-day Coffee Cake

12-16 Servings

Sebastian Maniscalco, (comedian) says, "Listen, nobody touch this cake, this is for company only, those crap muffins? Those are for you people." Hilarious but true! Similarly, this coffee cake is yummy old school, just in case the doorbell rings.

Please note: If you are not baking for vegans, you can use organic eggs.

3 EF eggs or 4 eggs
2 1/2 C beet sugar
4 tsp vanilla
1/2 C + 4 Tbs almond oil
2 C almond milk
5 C GF flour
2 Tbs baking powder
1/4 tsp salt
1 Tbs coffee beans

- Preheat oven to 350 degrees, oil a rectangular baking dish.

- In a mixer, add eggs, sugar, vanilla, oil and milk, mix.

- In a bowl, add flour, baking powder and salt.

- Add dry ingredients to the mixer, mix until all is combined.

- Pour into pan.

- Make crumb topping and sprinkle on top of cake and decorate with coffee beans.

- Bake 45-55 minutes (toothpick test)

Crumbs Topping

1 C GF flour
1 C brown sugar
1/2 C + 4Tbs almond oil
4 tsp cinnamon

- In mixer, add all ingredients, mix.

- For muffins, use a muffin tin with cupcake papers, pour batter in each 3/4 way up, and bake 35-45 minutes (toothpick test).

Carrot and Applesauce Cake

12-16 Servings

My mother-in-law taught me so much. I met Mary when I was 12. She was always in the kitchen whipping up something yummy. This is one of my favorites, this is my GF and DF version. I am so fortunate to have the original recipe in her handwriting, to pass on her legacy.

Please note: If you are not baking for vegans, you can use 4 organic eggs.

1 C almond oil
1+ 3/4 C beet sugar
3 EF eggs
3 C carrots, shredded
8 oz applesauce
1 C almond GF flour
1 + 1/4 C GF flour
1 tsp salt
2 tsp baking soda
2 tsp baking powder
2 tsp cinnamon

- Preheat oven to 350 degrees, oil & flour a Bunt pan.

- In a mixer, add the first 5 ingredients together, mix.

- In a bowl, add flours, salt, baking soda, baking powder and cinnamon.

- Add dry ingredients to the wet, slowly, mixing until combined.

- Pour into Bundt pan & bake 55 minutes (toothpick test).

- Cool 4 hours, run a knife around the middle tube and the side edges, put a plate onto the top and invert holding until cake releases.

Icing
8 oz DF cream cheese
1/2 C almond oil
2 C confectioner's sugar
1 &1/2 tsp Vanilla
1 Tbs, lemon rind, grated

- Mix all ingredients and spread over cooled cake and serve

- For muffins, use a muffin tin with cupcake papers, pour batter in each 3/4 way up, and bake 35-45 minutes (toothpick test).

Chocolate Fudge Cake

12-16 Servings

This is an incredible, rich and fancy dessert. My sister Celeste used to bring (her version) to every event. This is my New Year's Eve Cake. It freezes great. You just pull out of freezer and serve.

Please note: If you are not baking for vegans, you can use organic eggs.

2 bags, (24oz) DF dark chocolate chips
1 + 1/2 C almond oil
1 + 1/2 Tbs beet sugar
6 EF eggs
1+ 1/2 Tbs almond GF flour
1 Jar raspberry preserves (Optional)

- Preheat oven to 350 degrees, oil a springform pan.

- Melt chocolate. Using the bain marie method in procedures, or in the microwave by placing chopped chocolate in a microwave-safe bowl.

- Microwave in 30-second intervals, stirring between each, until chocolate is melted.

- In another glass or metal bowl, using a bain marie method: whip sugar, EF eggs, just until warm, 1 minute, remove from heat.

- In a mixer, whip sugar and egg mixture, until fluffy and add oil. Fold in flour and add cooled, melted chocolate mixture.

- Pour into springform pan, Bake 15 minutes.

- Immediately put in fridge on a towel. Cool completely, 1 hour.

- Remove from fridge, spread 1/2 jar of jam over top, run a knife around the pan edges, to loosen spring form.

- Move to a decorative plate and serve.

Fruits and Vegetables Bathed in Chocolate

Makes Many

Everything tastes better with chocolate. Make and tray all these chocolate gems for a fabulous presentation. The chili peppers are a unique addition, only for the brave. This is a great fun activity to do with children. Amount of chocolates will vary.

2 Bags vegan, dark chocolate pieces or chips
Coconut oil
Pineapple, slices
Strawberries, whole
Dried apricots
Dried jack fruit
Dried bananas
Dried ginger
Pecans/nuts
Potato chips, thick
Celery & peanut butter
Chili peppers
GF & DF graham crackers

- Wash and completely dry the fruit and vegetables.

- Melt chocolate. Using the bain marie method in procedures or in the microwave by placing the chopped chocolate in a microwave-safe bowl; microwave in 30-second intervals, stirring between each, until chocolate is melted.

- If your chocolate is very thick, add a 1 tsp of coconut oil.

- Line a sheet pan with parchment paper.Dip half the fruit, nuts or vegetable into the melted chocolate and then place on pan.

- Place in fridge to set for 30 minutes. Serve on a tray.

Gogi Ambrosia

10-12 Servings

A delicious, refreshing dessert, serve cold. Make a few hours ahead for chilling purposes. If using canned products, drain well. Preferably, no sugar added varieties. This recipe uses the following recipe for Nilla Pudding. Make Nilla pudding ahead, so it is ready. The fold method is used here, as it is gentler than mixing. The goal is to not break the fruit.

2 C Pineapple, crushed
2 C Mandarin oranges
1 C Cherries, pitted
2 Cans DF whipped cream
8 oz DF yogurt
16 oz Nilla Pudding (below)
8 oz sweet coconut flakes
1-3 tsp Gogi berry powder
2 1/2 C vegan marshmallows

- In a large bowl, with a spatula, fold together the whipped cream and the Yogurt.

- Fold in, gogi berry powder,1 tsp at a time until color and taste is to your preference.

- Add pineapple, orange segments and the cherries, fold.

- Add the Nilla Pudding and coconut flakes, fold.

- Refrigerate overnight or for a few hours, before serving.

- Add the marshmallows just before serving.

- Serve in a fancy bowl or bar glasses.

Nilla Pudding

Makes about 3 Cups

A versatile dessert, use in Gogi Ambrosia as a cake filling, or just eat as is. You can cover and keep in fridge for up to 2 weeks. I make this the day before, and it will become very thick. If chocolate is your desire, add 1 C of dark chocolate chips to hot milk mixture after bubbles appear.

1 (13oz) can (full fat) coconut milk
1 1/4 cups almond milk
4 Tbsp Arrowroot flour
1/3 C beet sugar
1 tsp vanilla extract
1/8 tsp salt
2 Tbs chai seeds (optional)

- In a medium pot, on medium heat, mix, arrowroot, and sugar.

- Mix in both milks and Chai seeds (continue to mix to avoid a burnt bottom), when bubbles appear, reduce heat to a low (total time is about 2 minutes to thicken pudding).

- Turn off heat, add vanilla and salt. Mix well!

- Transfer to a medium size bowl, cover with parchment paper, make sure it touches the top of pudding (this will prevent a pudding skin from forming, if pudding skin does form, it can be removed and discarded).

- Refrigerate until cold. It can take up to 24 hours to thicken completely.

- Pudding should be thick.

- Use in Gogi Ambrosia.

Key Lime Frozen Pie

6-8 Servings

This is my son and World Class Rower Tobin's favorite dessert. This version is frozen, a lighter tart and very refreshing. Living in Florida, I grew my own key limes. Start early in the day or the day ahead! It needs about 6 hours to freeze. Using a Magic Bullet will make it smooth. I use the entire lime. It's easy, adds additional tartness along with nutritious bioflavonoids.

2 C GF graham cracker crumbs
1/2 C Vegan butter, softened
1 C cashews, raw
8 Key limes or 4 limes
Lime, zest of 1 lime
3/4 C almond DF creamer
3/4 C beet sugar

- Soak cashews in filtered room temp water, enough to cover, for 2 hours.

- Preheat oven to 375 degrees, oil a pie plate.

- In a mixer, add graham crackers, mix until ground. Add 1/4 C of the butter, mix (should be gritty in texture).

- Remove with clean hands and press crumbs into pie plate and up the sides. Bake for 10 minutes or until golden brown. Remove from oven and cool on counter.

- With a sharp knife remove all the lime skins.

- Drain the cashews. In a food processor, or bullet, add cashews, limes, zest, creamer and sugar blend until smooth, 30 seconds.

- Pour filling into graham cracker crumb pie plate.

- Freeze for 6 hours, until firm.

- Remove from freezer, thaw a bit before serving like a pie.

Lemon and Mint Tea Cake

12-16 Servings

This cake is so light! It reminds me of a visit to England. All you need is a pot of tea. The original recipe is made with basil, though the mint was so refreshing and brings out its spring flavors. I encourage you to try both options. You can also use this recipe to make cupcakes, bake them for 20-30 minutes, cooled and then top with icing.

Please note: If you are not baking for vegans, you can use organic eggs.

1 C almond oil
2 C beet sugar
4 EF eggs or 6 eggs
2 C lemon DF yogurt
2 lemons, Juiced
2 lemons, zest
1/4 tsp lemon extract
20-30 leaves mint, sliced
3 C GF flour
3 tsp baking powder
1+ 1/2 tsp baking soda
1/2 tsp salt
1 Jar lemon jam

- Preheat oven to 350 degrees, oil a 9" springform pan.

- In mixer, add first 8 ingredients.

- In bowl, mix flour, baking powder, baking soda and salt.

- Add dry mixture to wet ingredients, mix.

- Pour into pan and bake for 50 minutes (toothpick test).

- Cool. Run a knife around springform pan to release cake and remove.

- In a bowl, add lemon jam and a touch of water mix, until blended. For the icing, apply to top, decorate with lemon rind and herbs, serve.

- For muffins, use a muffin tin with cupcake papers, pour batter in each 3/4 way up, and bake 35-45 minutes (toothpick test).

Molasses Ginger Cookies

24 Cookies

My kids love these! Great flavor!

Please note: If you are not baking for vegans, you can use organic eggs.

3/4 C vegan butter, softened.
1 C beet sugar
1/4 C dark molasses
1 EF egg
2 + 1/4 C GF flour
1 tsp baking soda
2 tsp ginger powder
3/4 tsp cinnamon
1/2 tsp cloves, ground
1/4 tsp salt
Beet sugar (for topping)

- Preheat oven to 350 degrees, oil a cookie sheet.

- In a mixer, add first 4 wet ingredients, mix well.

- In a bowl, mix together the dry ingredients.

- Slowly add dry to wet ingredients.

- Make cookies by rolling into balls (1" balls), use clean hands, similar to rolling play dough, with both palms. Put some sugar in a bowl. Take each ball and roll in sugar.

- Place each ball on a cookie sheet 2" apart, as they will rise and spread out.

- Bake 8 minutes for soft or 12 minutes crisp.

Peanut Butter and Chocolate Balls

24 Balls

This is my massage therapist, Deborah's recipe. Easy enough for kids to make. These ingredients marry and they are too good! The challenge for the at home cook is dipping the balls. Store for weeks in fridge.

2 C peanut butter
2 C confectioner's sugar
1/2 C of vegan butter, softened
2 C DF & GF graham crackers, crumbs or ground crackers
1 bag 12 oz DF chocolate chips
Coconut oil

- Line a cookie sheet with parchment paper.

- In a mixer, blend all ingredients together.

- Refrigerate 1 hour.

- With clean hands, roll dough into balls.

- Melt chocolate. Using the bain marie method in procedures or in the microwave by placing chopped chocolate in a microwave-safe bowl; microwave in 30-second intervals, stirring between each, until chocolate is melted. Add some oil if too thick.

- With a spoon, dip the balls in the chocolate, until coated. Place on oiled plate or cookie sheet, place back in fridge for 1 hour.

- *Please note: when removing from sheet, if you don't like the flat bottom, you can re-dip them.

- Serve or store in fridge.

Pear and Almond Tart

12-16 Servings

Pears are a delicious fruit but are always upstaged by other fruits. Nutritious fiber, antioxidants ,Vitamin C, K, potassium and copper. Please Allow 1-4 hours fridge time or dough can be made day before for firming stage.

Please note: If you are not baking for vegans, you can use organic eggs.

½ C+ powdered sugar
1/4 C sliced almonds
¼ tsp salt
1 EF egg
1/2 C vegan butter, softened
1¼ C GF flour

- Oil a tart pan (preferably with a removable bottom).

- In a food processor, grind powdered sugar, almonds, and salt. Add butter, EF egg and flour. Pulse until clumpy.

- With clean hands transfer dough to tart pan press into pan and up sides about 1/4". Seal any cracks with wet hands, refrigerate 1-4 hours.

Almond Filling

3/4 C almonds
1 Tbs GF flour
1/4 C beet sugar

1 Tbs maple syrup
1/3 C almond oil
1 EF egg
1/8 tsp salt

- In food processor, add almonds first, grind, then the rest of the ingredients and blend until smooth. Place in small bowl, refrigerate 1-4 hours.

Pears

4 C water
1¼ cups beet sugar
1½ Tbs lemon juice
3 firm pears, peeled

- In a pot, bring water, sugar and juice to a boil, mix in pears, cover and simmer until very tender, turning once, ~ 20 minutes. Turn off heat and drain water. Cool pears.

- Cut pears in half, remove core and stem, slice thin.

Assemble:

- Preheat oven to 350°F.

- Remove items from fridge.

- Pierce crust all over with a fork.

- Bake crust, about 25 minutes, until golden brown.

- Remove crust from oven and spread almond filling evenly in crust.

- Add pears, overlapping to create a fan or a nice design affect.

- Bake 55 minutes (toothpick test).

- Cool tart on rack, release sides from bottom of tart pan.

- Serve on a plate and dust with powdered sugar.

Wild Blueberry Pie

10-12 Servings

An Italian fruit tart. Very rustic looking! Use wild blueberries whenever possible. A super-fruit, rich in anthocyanin, a flavonoid with potent antioxidant capacity.

Blueberries
2 C wild blueberries
1 Tbs lemon juice, fresh
1/3 C beet sugar
4 tsp cornstarch

• Preheat oven to 375 degrees, oil a pie plate.

• In a bowl, add blueberries, juice, sugar and cornstarch.

• Mix well. Refrigerate for 30 minutes.

Crust
Please follow Universal Pie Crust page 79.

Pie filling
6 oz DF cream cheese, softened

• Spread the cream cheese in a thin layer, over the universal piecrust.

• Add the blueberry mixture into the piecrust, covering the cream cheese.

Finishing Wash
1 Tbs filtered water
1Tbs sugar, beaten

- Mix the water and the sugar.

- Brush the edges and sides of the crust with the wash.

- Bake for 30-45 minutes or until golden brown.

- Cool pie and serve warm or refrigerate until cold.

I hope you enjoyed cooking and baking from your heart!

A big loving *thankyou* to all my readers!

Please look out for more recipes, information
and yes, pictures on social media.

Vivienne Pasqua (McGee)
onemealforall.com